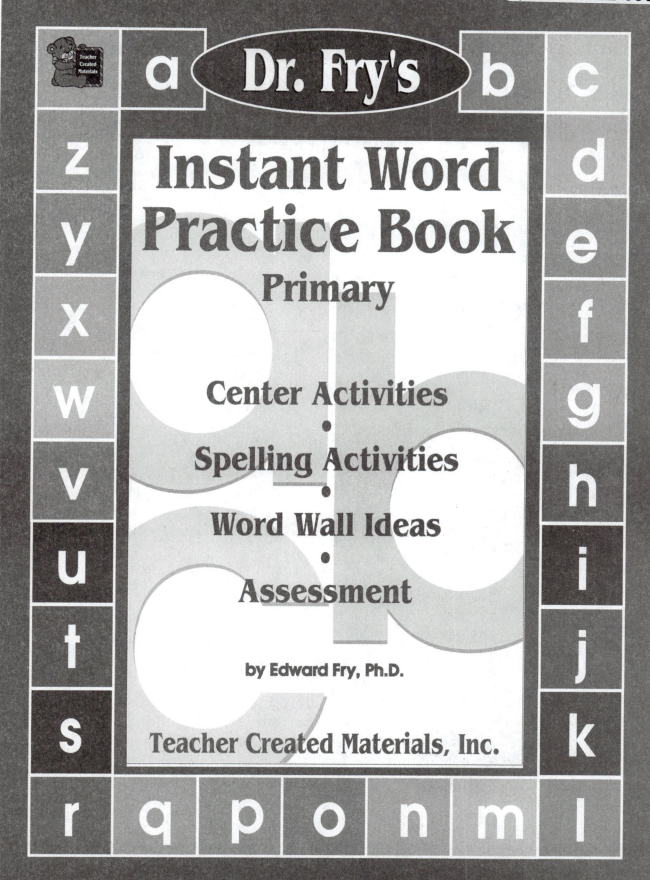

Dr. Fry's

a b c d e f g h i j k l m n o p q r s t u v w x y z

Instant Word Practice Book

Primary

Center Activities
·
Spelling Activities
·
Word Wall Ideas
·
Assessment

by Edward Fry, Ph.D.

Teacher Created Materials, Inc.

Instant Word Practice Book

Primary

by Edward Fry, Ph.D.

Editor
Lori Kamola, M.S. Ed.

Managing Editor
Karen Goldfluss, M.S. Ed.

Editor-in-Chief
Sharon Coan, M.S. Ed.

Illustrator
Ken Tunell

Art Coordinator
Denice Adorno

Cover Artist
Jamie Sochin

Product Manager
Phil Garcia

Imaging
James Edward Grace
Rosa C. See

Publishers
Rachelle Cracchiolo, M.S. Ed.
Mary Dupuy Smith, M.S. Ed.

Teacher Created Materials, Inc.
6421 Industry Way
Westminster, CA 92683
www.teachercreated.com

ISBN 0-7439-3503-9

©2001 Teacher Created Materials, Inc.
Reprinted, 2003
Made in U.S.A.

Table of Contents

Table of Contents *(cont.)*

Table of Contents (cont.)

Unit 7: some, her, would, make, like, him, into, time, has, look

Unit 8: two, more, write, go, see, number, no, way, could, people

Unit 9: my, than, first, water, been, call, who, oil, now, find

Table of Contents *(cont.)*

Table of Contents *(cont.)*

Table of Contents *(cont.)*

Table of Contents *(cont.)*

Table of Contents *(cont.)*

Table of Contents *(cont.)*

Table of Contents (cont.)

About This Book

The word puzzles and activities in this book are designed to reinforce Dr. Fry's Instant Word list. Classroom teachers, reading teachers, and special education teachers will all find these materials beneficial for their students. The reproducible puzzles and activity sheets can be used to supplement your reading program and other commercial materials. You may find that some of the pages are also useful in preparing students to take standardized tests.

The section called "How to Use This Book" discusses procedures for introducing the Instant Words to students and for using the various types of activities in this book. You will find it helpful to read through the entire section before using the materials with your students.

The Instant Words

The Instant Words comprise the most important words for reading and writing in the English language. It is absolutely impossible to read or write anything without knowing at least some of these words. The word list is based on research that revealed that 50 percent of all written material is composed of just the first 100 Instant Words. The first 300 Instant Words make up 65 percent of all written material. For further information on this list, see "The New Instant Word List" by Edward Fry, in the December 1980 issue of *The Reading Teacher.*

Students must recognize these words instantly for reading fluency and must spell them rapidly and correctly for writing fluency. Students need and learn many subject matter words as well, like "monster" or "helicopter," but the Instant Words are a core vocabulary.

This list is for beginning readers of any age—children or adults. The whole list is usually not mastered until beginning third-grade reading ability is achieved, although some students master it much earlier and others later.

The Instant Words also make an excellent spelling list. If you want more Instant Words, you can find 1,000 of them in *Dr. Fry's 1000 Instant Words* (TCM 2757).

Teaching Strategies

Teachers should be aware that the supplemental reading and writing activities cover three years of ability range. Don't rush a student through these activities. Take plenty of time for oral and silent story reading, comprehension instruction, phonics lessons, and a variety of activities for teaching students to read.

Be flexible and let some students or groups go through the activities more rapidly than others. Though a strong feature of these activities is their suggested sequence, you are free to omit or repeat selected activities or even skip students ahead. Many of the activities can be used in language arts centers; the directions can be laminated so they can be reused. You are the director of the most important overall activity, teaching reading.

How to Use This Book

Prior to beginning a unit, you should introduce the words reinforced by that unit. The number of words to be introduced at one time depends on the ability of the students. For students already familiar with some of the words, you may prefer to introduce all 10 words at once. On the other hand, some students may not be able to handle more than two or three new words at a time. Regardless of the number of words presented on a given day, all 10 words of a unit should be introduced before the students are asked to complete any of the written activities in that unit.

A number of the Instant Words have multiple meanings. In some cases, both meanings of a word are used. Therefore, you should look over the pages of each new unit to be certain that any multiple meanings are taken into consideration when the words are introduced to the students.

The following procedure can be used for introducing each word:

1. Write the word on the board or on heavy paper so that it can be added to your word wall.

2. Point to the word and pronounce it clearly and distinctly. Then have the students repeat the word several times as you point to it. Finally, call on various students to say the word.

3. Say the word again and then spell it, pointing to each letter as you say its name. Then have the students say the word and spell it as you point to each letter.

4. Use the word orally in a sentence or phrase. Then write on the board a sentence or phrase containing the word. This sentence could be written on chart paper so that it can be saved and reread at a later time. Finally, read what you wrote, then have the students read it with you.

After a group of words has been introduced, the students should be given the opportunity to practice recognizing the words. The words can be written on flashcards and prominently displayed. Spare moments throughout the school day (before lunch, after lunch, etc.) can then be used to check individual students or the entire class on their ability to recognize the words. Reading specialists and other teachers who work with a number of different groups of students each day can integrate practice of these words with other activities during class sessions.

When you are ready to begin a unit, you have the option of beginning it with either the "Flashcards" page or the "Write the Words" page. Suggestions for using both of these types of pages appear later.

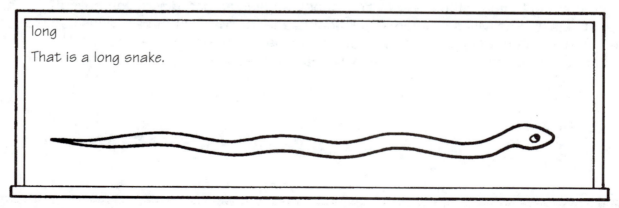

long

That is a long snake.

How to Use This Book *(cont.)*

Word Boxes

All of the pages in each unit contain word boxes; these boxes feature all 10 of the words reinforced in that unit. Before the students begin work on each work sheet, you should have them say the words in the word box. The words can also be written on the board, and you can call on various students to read them. This repetition is needed in order for the students to retain the words.

Fry's Instant Word Criterion Test

This test can be used to assess a child's knowledge of the 300 Instant Words. The teacher's record sheet has sections to record both spelling and word recognition skills. The test is useful for keeping a record of a child's knowledge and for reporting.

Progress Chart

Included in this book is a Progress Chart that can be used to keep track of the progress of each student. Students often find it motivating to keep records of their own progress. As each unit is completed, the chart can be filled in with scores or it can be used as a simple record of completion chart. The chart also gives you a handy record that can be kept in a file folder.

Answer Keys

Answer keys are provided at the end of the book to facilitate correcting. You may want to have your students check some of the pages in class to provide additional practice in reading the words. It is important to check the student work pages soon after they have been completed in order for the corrections to be meaningful for the students.

Additional Verbs

Additional verbs (verbs not included in the Instant Words) listed below have been added to 12 of the units. The 12 extra verbs are accompanied by drawings. These drawings illustrate the action that is named by the verb. The first of these additional verbs appears in Unit 6. The students' attention should be directed to the pictures at the top of the page, as these extra verbs are used in the sentences that the students will read.

The additional verbs are:

Unit 6	Unit 9	Unit 12	Unit 15
climb	drink	fly	draw
Unit 18	**Unit 21**	**Unit 23**	**Unit 26**
jump	wash	sleep	ride
Unit 27	**Unit 28**	**Unit 29**	**Unit 30**
sit	listen	laugh	sing

How to Use This Book *(cont.)*

Additional Nouns

A total of 80 additional nouns (nouns not included in the 300 Instant Words) have been added to various activity pages throughout the book. Each of these nouns is accompanied by a picture at the top of the page. You should go over these words with the students before having them complete each page, and inform them that these words will appear in the sentences they are going to read. Therefore, if they come to a word in a sentence that they do not know, a good strategy is to look at the pictures and their labels to see if the unknown word is identified there.

The additional nouns are:

Unit 15: School Workers
teacher, bus driver, secretary, principal, custodian

Unit 16: Clothing
shirt, pants, dress, shoes, hat

Unit 17: Writing Tools
pen, pencil, crayon, typewriter, computer

Unit 18: Zoo Animals
elephant, giraffe, bear, tiger, monkey

Unit 19: Toys
ball, doll, train, game, skateboard

Unit 20: School Items
marker, scissors, paste, ruler, chalkboard

Unit 21: Growing Things
bush, flower, grass, corn, tomatoes

Unit 22: Outdoor Things
sun, moon, star, cloud, rain

Unit 23: Pets
cat, dog, rabbit, bird, fish

Unit 24: Workers
farmer, police officer, cook, doctor, nurse

Unit 25: Farm Animals
horse, cow, pig, chicken, duck

Unit 26: Transportation
bicycle, truck, bus, plane, boat

Unit 27: Furniture
table, chair, sofa, chest, desk

Unit 28: Entertainment
television, radio, movie, ballgame, band

Unit 29: Eating Objects
cup, plate, bowl, fork, spoon

Unit 30: Buildings
store, gas station, church, theater, barn

How to Use This Book (cont.)

Directions for Using the "Flashcards" Pages

The flashcards for each unit can be cut out and retained by the students for use in a variety of activities. A set of the words could be copied on heavy paper and laminated to be used at a center as well. Suggested activities include the following:

1. **Peer Tutoring.** One child can hold up a word for the other children in a small group (or an individual child) to read. This activity can be made more interesting if the tutor flashes the card by turning it over quickly or briefly exposing it from behind a book. Students who miss words can later be given more practice. Also, flashcards from several units can be combined. For more durability, duplicate or photocopy the flashcards on heavy paper.

2. **Tachistoscope.** Flashcard pages can be reproduced on heavy paper and cut up the middle. The word strips can then be used in teacher-made (or student-made) tachistoscopes. A tachistoscope is a tool for showing one word for a very brief period of time. Heavy paper works well for this: make a holder to fit around the word strips with a cutout large enough to show one word at a time. The word strips should be able to slide through the tachistoscope vertically (see diagram).

3. **Know and Don't Know Piles.** An individual student can sort through a group of flashcards placing the known words in a "Know" pile and the unknown words in a "Don't Know" pile. Later a tutor can check to see if the "Know" words are indeed known and can help the student with the words in the "Don't Know" pile.

4. **Board Games.** Flashcards can also be used with either commercial or teacher-made (or sometimes student-made) board games. The boards can have a theme of race cars, horses, boats, and so forth. Typically a board features a track with spaces. A student throws dice or spins a spinner and moves a marker the indicated number of spaces if the word on the flashcard pile is correctly read. If the student does not read the word correctly, the turn is lost.

How to Use This Book *(cont.)*

5. **Word Endings.** Word endings can be added to many of the flashcards to create new words. These endings can be added to some of the words in Units 1–10: -s, -ing, -ed. These endings are commonly used with some of the words in Units 11–30: -s, -ing, -ed, -er, -ly, -est. Labels with word endings can be made and the flashcards can be sorted into word ending categories. You may choose to use the flashcards as an introduction to each unit. They may, however, be used at any time. The flashcards also provide an excellent review of words taught in earlier lessons, so students should be instructed to save the cards.

new	er

new	est

6. **Concentration.** Two students can pair up with two sets of flashcards and lay them face down in a mixed-up order. Each player turns over two cards. If they are a pair, he or she keeps them; if they are not, then they must be put back in exactly the same place, face down. The trick of the game is to remember the location of the cards so that one can make a pair with each two cards turned up. The student must read aloud each card when it is turned over. The other player may help read the words, if necessary.

7. **Bingo.** Students can be given blank word cards (page 19) with spaces five across and five down, and the students can fill in the spaces with their instant words. The teacher needs to direct the students to use certain units; for example, use any of the words from Units 1 through 3. The students can fill in the bingo cards with the words in any order. The teacher puts a set of flashcards in a basket and chooses one at a time to call out. The students can use any type of marker (e.g., tiles, beans, cubes) to cover the spaces. The teacher can determine if bingo will be called when a horizontal, vertical, or diagonal line—or even the entire board—is covered. The teacher can choose to show the words or write them on the board as they are called out to aid students with identifying the words.

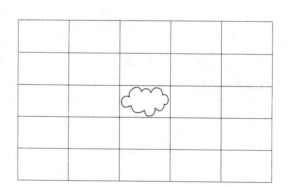

Bingo Game Card

How to Use This Book (cont.)

Directions for Using the "Write the Words" Pages

The purpose of these pages is to provide students with practice in recognizing the letter sequence of the words in each unit. While writing a word, a student's attention is automatically directed toward the letters and their sequence.

Before the students write the words in their proper spaces, they can write them with their fingers in the air. After completing the page, the students can take out a blank sheet of paper and write the words a second time using this procedure: (1) study a word on the "Write the Words" page, (2) write the word (from memory) on the second sheet of paper, and (3) check the newly written word by referring back to the original page.

It is recommended that students use manuscript (printing) rather than cursive when they complete the "Write the Words" pages. This procedure allows for greater attention to the individual letters in the words. Also, when students later meet these words in other contexts, the words will be printed rather than written in cursive.

Directions for Using the "Find the Words" Pages

To complete these pages, the students search for the hidden words in the puzzles and circle them. The Level B "Find the Words" puzzles are more difficult than the Level A puzzles. The words in the Level A puzzles all appear horizontally, whereas in the Level B puzzles words appear horizontally (left to right only), vertically (top to bottom only), or diagonally (left to right only, slanting down).

Some students may be confused by little words that are part of a bigger word (for example, he—the) or by a word that inadvertently appears in a puzzle but is not one of the words introduced in that unit. Therefore, you should instruct your students to look for and circle only the 10 Instant Words that are reinforced in the unit in which the puzzle appears.

Directions for Using the "Match Sentences with Pictures" Pages

(Units 1–10)

On these pages, the students are required to read each sentence and draw a line to the picture that best illustrates what the sentence is about.

Before the students begin work on a page, you should read the directions to them. Then students should read the words in the word box and complete the activity. After students complete a page, they should reread the sentences to make certain that they chose the proper picture for each sentence. In the early units, it is possible for students to respond correctly to some of the items by reading only the noun in the sentence. Therefore, you may wish to assess your students' recognition of the Instant Words in the unit by having them read the sentences orally when they have completed the page.

How to Use This Book (cont.)

Directions for Using the "Match Pictures with Sentences" Pages

(Units 11–20)

To complete these pages, the students will read both sentences beside each picture and will then choose the sentence that better describes or tells about what is shown in the picture. They will draw a line from the picture to the sentence they select.

After you read the directions and have the students say the words in the word box and the words under the pictures, you should then stress the importance of reading both sentences in their entirety before selecting the one that goes with the picture. In many cases, there exists only a slight difference between the two sentences. Therefore, careful reading is necessary.

When the students have completed their work, they should read over the sentences a final time to check the accuracy of their choices. You may wish to have the students check their papers by calling on various students to read the sentences they have chosen.

Directions for Using the "Write the Words in Sentences" Pages

(Units 21–30)

These pages provide students with practice in writing the words in sentences. Students are to read each sentence and select a word from the word box to complete the sentence. After they write the word in the space, they should then reread the sentence in its entirety to make certain that they have selected a word that makes sense in the context of the sentence. Some students may get confused and select words that appear under the pictures on some of the pages. They should be cautioned to select only the words that appear in the word box.

Directions for Using the "Choose the Correct Words" Pages

The number of words used on these pages differs slightly among the units. In Units 1–20, the students are to complete the sentences by selecting from two words printed directly below the writing spaces. Units 21–30 have three word choices below each sentence.

Students will (1) read a sentence and select the best word to complete that sentence, (2) write the selected word in the space, and (3) reread the sentence to check the accuracy of their choices.

How to Use This Book (cont.)

Directions for Using the "Just-for-Fun" Pages

A "Just-for-Fun" page is included at the end of each unit. These pages provide additional practice with the words presented in that unit. Five types of "Just-for-Fun" pages are included; suggestions for their use follow.

Word Scramble

On the "Word Scramble" pages, the words from the unit have been scrambled. The students are to put the letters of each word back in their proper order by correctly writing the word on the line beside its scrambled form. To simplify the procedure, they can cross off each word in the word box as they use it.

Pages of this type can be difficult for young children or children of limited ability. For students who have a difficult time with this task, try having them use letter tiles that represent the scrambled letters so they can physically manipulate the letters to unscramble them. If your students still have difficulty with these pages, the pages can be completed as a group activity, or they can be omitted entirely.

Missing Letters

The words on the "Missing Letters" pages all have one letter missing. The students will fill in the missing letters to spell the words from the word box. They will then copy the entire word on the line below its corresponding picture.

As an extension of this activity, some students may enjoy creating a "Missing Letters" page for their classmates to complete.

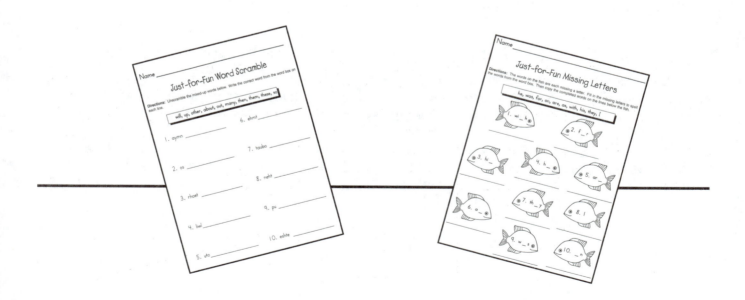

How to Use This Book (cont.)

Anagrams

The "Anagrams" pages contain the letters needed to spell the words from the unit in which the page appears. The students should cut out the letters and spread them out on their desks.

To avoid confusion, letters that might be reversed by the students (for example, **u** and **n**) have lines printed under them. Students should be told that when the line is at the bottom, the letter is right side up.

After the students have cut out the letters, they can arrange them to spell the Instant Words reinforced by that unit. They can either spell each word as you pronounce it or they can spell the words independently by selecting them from the word box. If students are to spell each word by looking at it in the word box, they should be instructed to use care when cutting out the letters and not to throw away the portion of the page containing the word box.

Mystery Words

To complete the "Mystery Word" activities, students use the code symbols to match the letters. The code symbols for each letter of the alphabet are shown in a box on the page for the students to use. The letter is written by the student on the line above the symbol. Each of the 10 instant words is written in code for the students to solve.

Letter Squares

On these pages, each word from the word box is missing one or more letters. The students will spell the words by writing the missing letters in the squares. After they have completed a word, they should copy it on the line below the squares. Your students may find this activity is easier if they cross off the words in the word box as they use them.

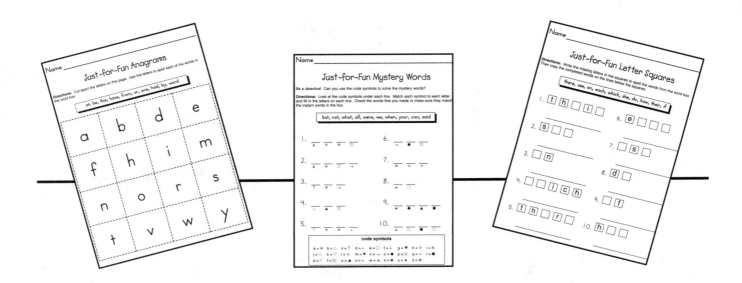

How to Use This Book *(cont.)*

Directions for Continued Reinforcement/Review

As was noted earlier, the flashcards can be retained by the students and used to review words from previous units. Also, the "Know/Don't Know" activity described earlier can be expanded into a word-bank in which students keep their cards in a small box or word bank. The students should be periodically checked on the words in their banks to make certain that they have not forgotten previously learned words. Words that they don't know can be retaught.

Additional reinforcement can be provided by using the words in spelling, handwriting, creative writing, and other language arts lessons. Students are more likely to remember words if they are given frequent opportunities to use them.

If, after completing a number of units, you discover that many of the students do not seem to remember previously taught words, some additional review and reteaching may be necessary. As these units build on each other, with each new unit containing words from previous units, students can become lost if they do not adequately learn the words from those earlier units. It is a fact that some students require more exposure to words than other students in order to master those words. For these students, it may be necessary to repeat entire units. The goal should be to help the students learn the words, not simply to cover the material.

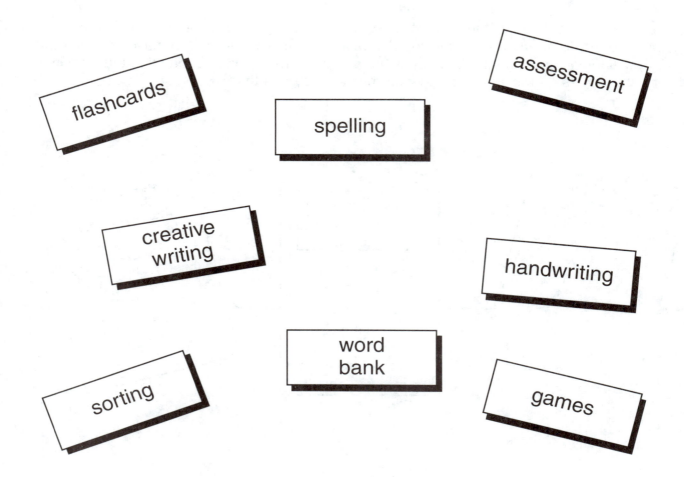

Fry's Instant Word Criterion Test

The test on the following pages can save you a lot of time by testing a child's knowledge of the 300 Instant Words. Teach only what the child doesn't know. To find out which words the child knows, have him or her read from one copy of the test while you check each known word on your copy of the test.

In order to save even more time, use the Quick Survey Test first. This test is the first three words of each column. Ask the child to read all the words in the Quick Survey Test for a page (not the whole 100 words on the page). If the child knows all the words in the Quick Survey, you can assume that he or she knows most of the words on that page, so you can then go on to the next page.

If the child makes two or more mistakes, you should test the whole page. As you can see from looking at the test, there are 10 words in each unit. If the child makes a mistake in any unit, then you can use the activities in this book to teach the words in that unit.

This Instant Word Criterion Test is useful for keeping a record of a child's knowledge and for reporting. You might want to keep a copy of the test in each child's folder so that you can test-teach-test-teach, and so forth. In other words, you can test until you find a weakness, teach the words and have the child complete the unit, then test again to find the next weakness.

Fry's Instant Word Criterion Test also makes an excellent record of progress. You might want to administer it at the beginning of the year, then in the middle of the year, and again at the end of the year, to show progress. A record of accomplishment will help you at report-card time and in parent conferences.

This is a criterion test, which means that it measures a child's knowledge against a criterion—in this case, the criterion is the 300 Instant Words. The criterion test tells you how well a child is progressing toward a criterion—in other words, how much of the subject matter the child knows. Criterion tests such as this one also suggest what should be taught next.

Fry's Instant Word Criterion Test will work well with beginning readers of any age: young children, remedial reading or special education students (both elementary and secondary), or illiterate adults. It will also help you to individualize instruction in your class: each student or small group can be working on a different unit of the activities.

The criterion test can also be used as a spelling assessment tool. The child can be asked to spell each word in written form, and this information can be recorded on the teacher's checklist as well. There are two lines next to each word to record the student answers. Use different colored pens to check off the words for spelling and word recognition. For example, use green for spelling and blue for word recognition. It is important for students to be able to read the words and, eventually, spell them correctly.

Name_____

Fry's Instant Word Criterion Test
First Hundred

Quick Survey Test of Words in Units 1–10

Unit 1   **Unit 6**

1. ___ ___ the   26. ___ ___ or   51. ___ ___ will   76. ___ ___ number

2. ___ ___ of   27. ___ ___ one   52. ___ ___ up   77. ___ ___ no

3. ___ ___ and   28. ___ ___ had   53. ___ ___ other   78. ___ ___ way

4. ___ ___ a   29. ___ ___ by   54. ___ ___ about   79. ___ ___ could

5. ___ ___ to   30. ___ ___ word   55. ___ ___ out   80. ___ ___ people

6. ___ ___ in   **Unit 4**   56. ___ ___ many   **Unit 9**

7. ___ ___ is   31. ___ ___ but   57. ___ ___ then   81. ___ ___ my

8. ___ ___ you   32. ___ ___ not   58. ___ ___ them   82. ___ ___ than

9. ___ ___ that   33. ___ ___ what   59. ___ ___ these   83. ___ ___ first

10. ___ ___ it   34. ___ ___ all   60. ___ ___ so   84. ___ ___ water

Unit 2   35. ___ ___ were   85. ___ ___ been

11. ___ ___ he   36. ___ ___ we   **Unit 7**   86. ___ ___ call

12. ___ ___ was   37. ___ ___ when   61. ___ ___ some   87. ___ ___ who

13. ___ ___ for   38. ___ ___ your   62. ___ ___ her   88. ___ ___ oil

14. ___ ___ on   39. ___ ___ can   63. ___ ___ would   89. ___ ___ now

15. ___ ___ are   40. ___ ___ said   64. ___ ___ make   90. ___ ___ find

16. ___ ___ as   **Unit 5**   65. ___ ___ like   **Unit 10**

17. ___ ___ with   41. ___ ___ there   66. ___ ___ him   91. ___ ___ long

18. ___ ___ his   42. ___ ___ use   67. ___ ___ into   92. ___ ___ down

19. ___ ___ they   43. ___ ___ an   68. ___ ___ time   93. ___ ___ day

20. ___ ___ I   44. ___ ___ each   69. ___ ___ has   94. ___ ___ did

Unit 3   45. ___ ___ which   70. ___ ___ look   95. ___ ___ get

21. ___ ___ at   46. ___ ___ she   **Unit 8**   96. ___ ___ come

22. ___ ___ be   47. ___ ___ do   71. ___ ___ two   97. ___ ___ made

23. ___ ___ this   48. ___ ___ how   72. ___ ___ more   98. ___ ___ may

24. ___ ___ have   49. ___ ___ their   73. ___ ___ write   99. ___ ___ part

25. ___ ___ from   50. ___ ___ if   74. ___ ___ go   100. ___ ___ over

75. ___ ___ see

Name _____

Fry's Instant Word Criterion Test
Second Hundred

Quick Survey Test of Words in Units 11–20

Unit 11

101. ___ ___ new
102. ___ ___ sound
103. ___ ___ take

126. ___ ___ great
127. ___ ___ where
128. ___ ___ help

Unit 16

151. ___ ___ put
152. ___ ___ end
153. ___ ___ does

176. ___ ___ kind
177. ___ ___ hand
178. ___ ___ picture

---

104. ___ ___ only
105. ___ ___ little
106. ___ ___ work
107. ___ ___ know
108. ___ ___ place
109. ___ ___ year
110. ___ ___ live

Unit 12

111. ___ ___ me
112. ___ ___ back
113. ___ ___ give
114. ___ ___ most
115. ___ ___ very
116. ___ ___ after
117. ___ ___ thing
118. ___ ___ our
119. ___ ___ just
120. ___ ___ name

Unit 13

121. ___ ___ good
122. ___ ___ sentence
123. ___ ___ man
124. ___ ___ think
125. ___ ___ say

129. ___ ___ through
130. ___ ___ much

Unit 14

131. ___ ___ before
132. ___ ___ line
133. ___ ___ right
134. ___ ___ too
135. ___ ___ mean
136. ___ ___ old
137. ___ ___ any
138. ___ ___ same
139. ___ ___ tell
140. ___ ___ boy

Unit 15

141. ___ ___ follow
142. ___ ___ came
143. ___ ___ want
144. ___ ___ show
145. ___ ___ also
146. ___ ___ around
147. ___ ___ form
148. ___ ___ three
149. ___ ___ small
150. ___ ___ set

154. ___ ___ another
155. ___ ___ well
156. ___ ___ large
157. ___ ___ must
158. ___ ___ big
159. ___ ___ even
160. ___ ___ such

Unit 17

161. ___ ___ because
162. ___ ___ turn
163. ___ ___ here
164. ___ ___ why
165. ___ ___ ask
166. ___ ___ went
167. ___ ___ men
168. ___ ___ read
169. ___ ___ need
170. ___ ___ land

Unit 18

171. ___ ___ different
172. ___ ___ home
173. ___ ___ us
174. ___ ___ move
175. ___ ___ try

179. ___ ___ again
180. ___ ___ change

Unit 19

181. ___ ___ off
182. ___ ___ play
183. ___ ___ spell
184. ___ ___ air
185. ___ ___ away
186. ___ ___ animal
187. ___ ___ house
188. ___ ___ point
189. ___ ___ page
190. ___ ___ letter

Unit 20

191. ___ ___ mother
192. ___ ___ answer
193. ___ ___ found
194. ___ ___ study
195. ___ ___ still
196. ___ ___ learn
197. ___ ___ should
198. ___ ___ America
199. ___ ___ world
200. ___ ___ high

Fry's Instant Word Criterion Test
Third Hundred

Quick Survey Test of Words in Units 21–30

Unit 21
201. ___ ___ every
202. ___ ___ near
203. ___ ___ add

226. ___ ___ left
227. ___ ___ don't
228. ___ ___ few

Unit 26
251. ___ ___ until
252. ___ ___ children
253. ___ ___ side

276. ___ ___ idea
277. ___ ___ enough
278. ___ ___ eat

204. ___ ___ food
205. ___ ___ between
206. ___ ___ own
207. ___ ___ below
208. ___ ___ country
209. ___ ___ plant
210. ___ ___ last

Unit 22
211. ___ ___ school
212. ___ ___ father
213. ___ ___ keep
214. ___ ___ tree
215. ___ ___ never
216. ___ ___ start
217. ___ ___ city
218. ___ ___ earth
219. ___ ___ eye
220. ___ ___ light

Unit 23
221. ___ ___ thought
222. ___ ___ head
223. ___ ___ under
224. ___ ___ story
225. ___ ___ saw

229. ___ ___ while
230. ___ ___ along

Unit 24
231. ___ ___ might
232. ___ ___ close
233. ___ ___ something
234. ___ ___ seem
235. ___ ___ next
236. ___ ___ hard
237. ___ ___ open
238. ___ ___ example
239. ___ ___ begin
240. ___ ___ life

Unit 25
241. ___ ___ always
242. ___ ___ those
243. ___ ___ both
244. ___ ___ paper
245. ___ ___ together
246. ___ ___ got
247. ___ ___ group
248. ___ ___ often
249. ___ ___ run
250. ___ ___ important

254. ___ ___ feet
255. ___ ___ car
256. ___ ___ mile
257. ___ ___ night
258. ___ ___ walk
259. ___ ___ white
260. ___ ___ sea

Unit 27
261. ___ ___ began
262. ___ ___ grow
263. ___ ___ took
264. ___ ___ river
265. ___ ___ four
266. ___ ___ carry
267. ___ ___ state
268. ___ ___ once
269. ___ ___ book
270. ___ ___ hear

Unit 28
271. ___ ___ stop
272. ___ ___ without
273. ___ ___ second
274. ___ ___ late
275. ___ ___ miss

279. ___ ___ face
280. ___ ___ watch

Unit 29
281. ___ ___ far
282. ___ ___ Indian
283. ___ ___ real
284. ___ ___ almost
285. ___ ___ let
286. ___ ___ above
287. ___ ___ girl
288. ___ ___ sometimes
289. ___ ___ mountain
290. ___ ___ cut

Unit 30
291. ___ ___ young
292. ___ ___ talk
293. ___ ___ soon
294. ___ ___ list
295. ___ ___ song
296. ___ ___ leave
297. ___ ___ family
298. ___ ___ body
299. ___ ___ music
300. ___ ___ color

Name _____

Fry's Instant Word Criterion Test
First Hundred

Quick Survey Test of Words in Units 1–10

Unit 1

1. the
2. of
3. and

Unit 6

51. will
52. up
53. other

76. number
77. no
78. way

4. a
5. to
6. in
7. is
8. you
9. that
10. it

26. or
27. one
28. had
29. by
30. word

54. about
55. out
56. many
57. then
58. them
59. these
60. so

79. could
80. people

Unit 4

31. but
32. not
33. what
34. all
35. were
36. we
37. when
38. your
39. can
40. said

Unit 9

81. my
82. than
83. first
84. water
85. been
86. call
87. who
88. oil
89. now
90. find

Unit 2

11. he
12. was
13. for
14. on
15. are
16. as
17. with
18. his
19. they
20. I

Unit 7

61. some
62. her
63. would
64. make
65. like
66. him
67. into
68. time
69. has
70. look

Unit 5

41. there
42. use
43. an
44. each
45. which
46. she
47. do
48. how
49. their
50. if

Unit 10

91. long
92. down
93. day
94. did
95. get
96. come
97. made
98. may
99. part
100. over

Unit 3

21. at
22. be
23. this
24. have
25. from

Unit 8

71. two
72. more
73. write
74. go
75. see

Fry's Instant Word Criterion Test
Second Hundred

Quick Survey Test of Words in Units 11–20

Unit 11
101. new
102. sound
103. take

126. great
127. where
128. help

Unit 16
151. put
152. end
153. does

176. kind
177. hand
178. picture

---

104. only
105. little
106. work
107. know
108. place
109. year
110. live

Unit 12
111. me
112. back
113. give
114. most
115. very
116. after
117. thing
118. our
119. just
120. name

Unit 13
121. good
122. sentence
123. man
124. think
125. say

129. through
130. much

Unit 14
131. before
132. line
133. right
134. too
135. mean
136. old
137. any
138. same
139. tell
140. boy

Unit 15
141. follow
142. came
143. want
144. show
145. also
146. around
147. form
148. three
149. small
150. set

154. another
155. well
156. large
157. must
158. big
159. even
160. such

Unit 17
161. because
162. turn
163. here
164. why
165. ask
166. went
167. men
168. read
169. need
170. land

Unit 18
171. different
172. home
173. us
174. move
175. try

179. again
180. change

Unit 19
181. off
182. play
183. spell
184. air
185. away
186. animal
187. house
188. point
189. page
190. letter

Unit 20
191. mother
192. answer
193. found
194. study
195. still
196. learn
197. should
198. America
199. world
200. high

Fry's Instant Word Criterion Test
Third Hundred

Quick Survey Test of Words in Units 21–30

Unit 21
201. every
202. near
203. add

226. left
227. don't
228. few

Unit 26
251. until
252. children
253. side

276. idea
277. enough
278. eat

204. food
205. between
206. own
207. below
208. country
209. plant
210. last

229. while
230. along
Unit 24
231. might
232. close
233. something
234. seem
235. next
236. hard
237. open
238. example
239. begin
240. life

254. feet
255. car
256. mile
257. night
258. walk
259. white
260. sea
Unit 27
261. began
262. grow
263. took
264. river
265. four

279. face
280. watch
Unit 29
281. far
282. Indian
283. real
284. almost
285. let
286. above
287. girl
288. sometimes
289. mountain
290. cut

Unit 22
211. school
212. father
213. keep
214. tree
215. never
216. start
217. city
218. earth
219. eye
220. light

Unit 25
241. always
242. those
243. both
244. paper
245. together

266. carry
267. state
268. once
269. book
270. hear

Unit 30
291. young
292. talk
293. soon
294. list
295. song

Unit 23
221. thought
222. head
223. under
224. story
225. saw

246. got
247. group
248. often
249. run
250. important

Unit 28
271. stop
272. without
273. second
274. late
275. miss

296. leave
297. family
298. body
299. music
300. color

Name _____

Progress Chart

Color in or mark the box for each unit completed and enter the date of completion.

First Hundred Instant Words

Unit 1	Unit 2	Unit 3	Unit 4	Unit 5	Unit 6	Unit 7	Unit 8	Unit 9	Unit 10

Second Hundred Instant Words

Unit 11	Unit 12	Unit 13	Unit 14	Unit 15	Unit 16	Unit 17	Unit 18	Unit 19	Unit 20

Third Hundred Instant Words

Unit 21	Unit 22	Unit 23	Unit 24	Unit 25	Unit 26	Unit 27	Unit 28	Unit 29	Unit 30

Unit 1

Flashcards

Directions: Cut out the flashcards and use them to help you learn the words.

the, of, and, a, to, in, is, you, that, it

the	in
of	is
and	you
a	that
to	it

Name _____ 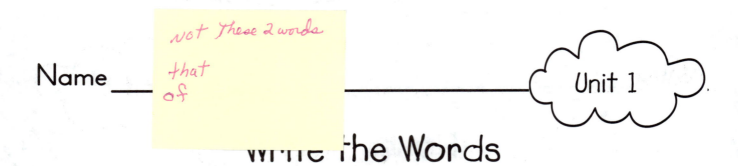 Unit 1

Write the Words

Directions: Write the words in the spaces.

the, of, and, a, to, in, is, you, that, it

1. the _____

the
_____

2. of _____

_____

3. and _____

_____

4. a _____

_____

5. to _____

_____

6. in _____

_____

7. is _____

_____

8. you _____

_____

9. that _____

_____

10. it _____

_____

Name _____

Find the Words—Level A

Directions: There are 10 Instant Words hidden here. Can you find and circle them?

Here are the words to look for:

a, in, it, that, to, and, is, of, the, you

Match Sentences with Pictures

Directions: Draw a line from each sentence to the picture it describes.

the, a, in, is, that, of, and, to, you, it

dog   cat   fish   bird   hat   car   rabbit   picture

1. The cat is in the car.

a.

2. A fish is in the hat.

b.

3. That is a picture of a dog and a rabbit.

c.

4. It is a fish and a bird.

d.

5. It is to you.

e.

6. That is a picture of a cat.

f.

Name _____  Unit 1

Find the Words—Level B

Directions: There are 10 Instant Words hidden here. Can you find and circle them?

Here are the words to look for:

a, in, it, that, to, and, is, of, the, you

```
B Z S I T J C V
T R A D F Y R D
I B X T W C O G
N L M H K E N U
C T Q E V R B J
Z A N D P Q I S
T K M V O F A N
J O G T H A T F
```

Name _____  Unit 1

Choose the Correct Words

Directions: Choose the correct word to complete each sentence and write the word in the space.

the, of, and, a, to, in, is, you, that, it

bird   cat   dog   fish   hat   picture

1. A bird is in _____ hat.
that of

2. It is a dog _____ a cat.
a and

3.  The cat is in _____ hat.
is the

4. That is a picture _____ a fish.
of to

5. It is to _____ .
and you

6. A bird is _____ the picture.
in it

Just-for-Fun Word Scramble

Directions: Unscramble the mixed-up words below. Write the correct word from the word box on each line. Use letter tiles if you need them.

the, of, and, a, to, in, is, you, that, it

1. si _____

2. atth _____

3. eht _____

4. ti _____

5. a _____

6. fo _____

7. dan _____

8. ni _____

9. uyo _____

10. ot _____

Name _____

Flashcards

Directions: Cut out the flashcards and use them to help you learn the words.

he, was, for, on, are, as, with, his, they, I

he	as
was	with
for	his
on	they
are	I

40

Name _____  Unit 2

Write the Words

Directions: Write the words in the spaces.

he, was, for, on, are, as, with, his, they, I

1. he _____

   he _____

2. was _____

   _____

3. for _____

   _____

4. on _____

   _____

5. are _____

   _____

6. as _____

   _____

7. with _____

   _____

8. his _____

   _____

9. they _____

   _____

10. I _____

    _____

Find the Words—Level A

Directions: There are 10 Instant Words hidden here. Can you find and circle them?

Here are the words to look for:

are, for, his, on, was, as, he, I, they, with

```
T  H  E  Y  Q  U  H
F  O  R  W  A  S  R
O  Q  A  R  E  K  I
C  E  H  E  H  F  F
L  R  D  W  I  T  H
C  R  B  Y  P  A  S
H  I  S  O  N  D  M
```

Name _____

Match Sentences with Pictures

Directions: Draw a line from each sentence to the picture it describes.

| he, for, are, with, they, was, on, as, his, I |

boy   girl   cat   car   dog

1. They are with the cat.

a.

2. The cat and I are on a car.

b.

3. It is his dog.

c.

4. The car is for the boy.

d.

5. The girl was in the car.

e.

6. The boy looked as the dog was
in the car.

f.

          #3503 Instant Word Practice Book

Name _____  Unit 2

Find the Words—Level B

Directions: There are 10 Instant Words hidden here. Can you find and circle them?

Here are the words to look for:

are, for, his, on, was, as, he, I, they, with

? ? ? ? ? ? ?

? H I S B O N D W ?

? F H W A S K N I ?

A P Q A C I V T

? S U Z D R X M H ?

M T X M K E R Z

? J C H S W Z F G ?

? H E Q E R H O B

L T R D Y L R S ?

? ? ? ? ? ? ?

Unit 2

Choose the Correct Words

Directions: Choose the correct word to complete each sentence and write the word in the space.

| he, was, for, on, are, as, with, his, they, I |

cat   chair

1. He _____ on the chair.
       was   with

2. They _____ on a chair.
         as   are

3. He is with _____ cat.
              for   his

4. _____ are with his cat.
   They   I

5. It is _____ that chair.
         he   on

6. It is _____ you.
         as   for

Name _____  Unit 2

Just-for-Fun Missing Letters

Directions: The words on the fish are each missing a letter. Fill in the missing letters to spell the words from the word box. Then copy the completed words on the lines below the fish.

he, was, for, on, are, as, with, his, they, I

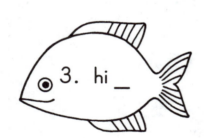

1. wi _ h

2. f _ r

_____   _____

3. hi _

4. h _

5. ar _

_____

_____   _____

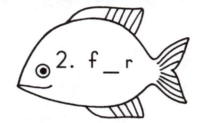

6. a _

7. th _ y

8. I

_____

_____   _____

9. w _ s

10. _ n

_____   _____

Unit 3

Flashcards

Directions: Cut out the flashcards and use them to help you learn the words.

at, be, this, have, from, or, one, had, by, word

at	or
be	one
this	had
have	by
from	word

Name _____

Unit 3

Write the Words

Directions: Write the words in the spaces.

| at, be, this, have, from, or, one, had, by, word |

1. at

____at____

2. be

3. this

4. have

5. from

6. or

7. one

8. had

9. by

10. word

Name _____

Find the Words–Level A

Directions: There are 10 Instant Words hidden here. Can you find and circle them?

Here are the words to look for:

be, from, have, or, word, at, by, had, one, this

```
J  E  O  N  E  B  E
A  T  H  I  S  T  M
W  S  P  X  B  Z  L
O  G  V  H  K  O  R
O  K  Z  F  R  O  M
H  A  V  E  H  A  D
B  Y  W  O  R  D  Z
```

Match Sentences with Pictures

Directions: Draw a line from each sentence to the picture it describes.

at, by, had, one, this, be, from, have, or, word

cow   duck   horse   pig   barn   boy

1. His horse is by this barn.   a.

2. They have one horse and one cow.   b.

3. He had a duck.   c.

4. Is this the word boy or the word pig?   d.

5. Is this from you?   e.

6. You have to be in the barn!   f.

Unit 3

Find the Words—Level B

Directions: There are 10 Instant Words hidden here. Can you find and circle them?

Here are the words to look for:

at, by, had, one, this, be, from, have, or, word

```
C B Y F H K M H
F P S B E V H A
Z R M O N E A D
T N O Q D S V R
H L T M J A E Z
I X R G L T A X
S W O R D J B O
E T W I N X C R
```

Choose the Correct Words

Directions: Choose the correct word to complete each sentence and write the word in the space.

at, be, this, have, from, or, one, had, by, word

man   cow   horse   pig   barn

1. I have to _____ this pig.
   have   be

2. The man had a horse _____ his barn.
   or   from

3. I have to _____ at the barn.
   by   be

4. Is this cow for you _____ for the man?
   or   one

5. One pig is _____ the cow.
   by   be

6. This is _____ word for you.
   had   one

Just-for-Fun Spelling

Directions: Cut apart the letters on this page. Use the letters to spell each of the words in the word box.

at, be, this, have, from, or, one, had, by, word

a	b	d	e
f	h	i	m
n	o	r	s
t	v	w	y

Name _____

Flashcards

Directions: Cut out the flashcards and use them to help you learn the words.

but, not, what, all, were, we, when, your, can, said

but	we
not	when
what	your
all	can
were	said

Name _____  Unit 4

Write the Words

Directions: Write the words in the spaces.

| but, not, what, all, were, we, when, your, can, said |

1. but

   but
   _____

2. not

   _____

3. what

   _____

4. all

   _____

5. were

   _____

6. we

   _____

7. when

   _____

8. your

   _____

9. can

   _____

10. said

   _____

Name _____  Unit 4

Find the Words—Level A

Directions: There are 10 Instant Words hidden here. Can you find and circle them?

Here are the words to look for:

all, can, said, were, when, but, not, we, what, your

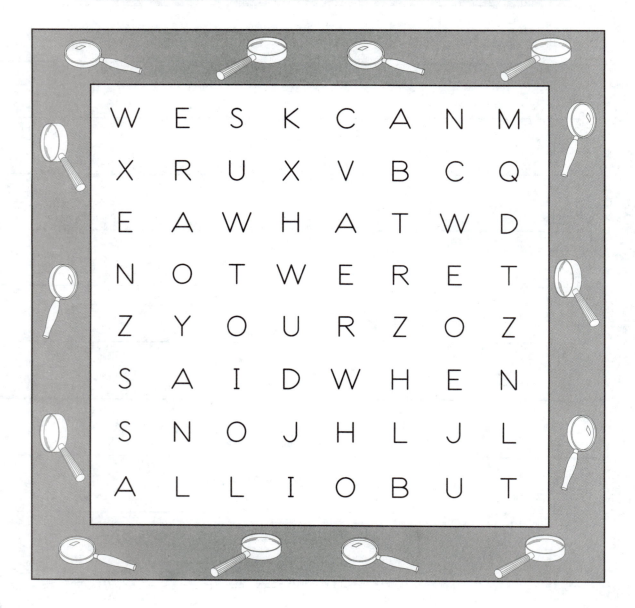

W E S K C A N M
X R U X V B C Q
E A W H A T W D
N O T W E R E T
Z Y O U R Z O Z
S A I D W H E N
S N O J H L J L
A L L I O B U T

Name _____  Unit 4

Match Sentences with Pictures

Directions: Draw a line from each sentence to the picture it describes.

not, all, when, can, said, but, what, were, we, your

girl   man   cow   duck   horse   boy   barn

1. We were at the barn but the cow was not.   a.

2. "Is that your horse?" said the boy.   b.

3. The duck can have all of it.   c.

4. The girl said, "When can I be on the horse?"   d.

5. The man said, "You can have this cow."   e.

6. "What can I have?" said the boy.   f.

Name _____

Unit 4

Find the Words—Level B

Directions: There are 10 Instant Words hidden here. Can you find and circle them?

Here are the words to look for:

all, can, said, were, when, but, not, we, what, your

W	B	N	O	T	Y	C	E	G
E	H	J	N	P	R	O	L	V
U	X	R	W	B	F	J	U	D
A	L	L	C	H	D	I	T	R
M	P	W	E	R	E	L	X	S
S	B	Z	C	D	Y	N	Q	C
R	U	Q	S	A	I	D	E	A
Y	T	M	A	W	H	A	T	N
O	Z	Q	F	W	I	K	O	T

Choose the Correct Words

Directions: Choose the correct word to complete each sentence and write the word in the space.

but, not, what, all, were, we, when, your, can, said

 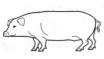

boy   duck   pig

1.   Is this _____ word?
   your   said

2.   You cannot have _____ of that.
   were   all

3.   The duck is in it _____ the pig is not.
   were   but

4.   _____ were all in it.
   We   What

5.  "When we _____ all in it, the duck was not,"
   you   were
   said the boy.

6.   _____ is that?
   When   What

Name _____

Unit 4

Just-for-Fun Mystery Words

Be a detective! Can you use the code symbols to solve the mystery words?

Directions: Look at the code symbols under each line. Match each symbol to each letter and fill in the letters on each line. Check the words that you made to make sure they match the instant words in the box.

but, not, what, all, were, we, when, your, can, said

1. ___ ___ ___ ___
   ◬   ⊙   ✳   ⊠

6. ___ ___ ___
   →   ●   ⊠

2. ___ ___ ___ ___
   ◬   ⊙   □   →

7. ___ ___ ___
   ✳   ☆   ☆

3. ___ ___ ___
   ↑   ✳   →

8. ___ ___
   ◬   □

4. ___ ___ ___
   △   ▲   ⊠

9. ___ ___ ___ ___
   ★   ●   ▲   ■

5. ___ ___ ___ ___
   ♡   ✳   ✕   ÷

10. ___ ___ ___ ___
    ◬   □   ■   □

Code Symbols

a = ✳   b = △   c = ↑   d = ÷   e = □   f = ↓   g = ▼   h = ⊙   i = ✕

j = ○   k = ▽   l = ☆   m = ♥   n = →   o = ●   p = ▫   q = ←   r = ■

s = ♡   t = ⊠   u = ▲   v = +   w = ◬   x = ✺   y = ★   z = ⊗

Flashcards

Directions: Cut out the flashcards and use them to help you learn the words.

there, use, an, each, which, she, do, how, their, if

there	she
use	do
an	how
each	their
which	if

Name _____  Unit 5

Write the Words

Directions: Write the words in the spaces.

there, use, an, each, which, she, do, how, their, if

1. there
   _____
   there
   _____

2. use
   _____

   _____

3. an
   _____

   _____

4. each
   _____

   _____

5. which
   _____

   _____

6. she
   _____

   _____

7. do
   _____

   _____

8. how
   _____

   _____

9. their
   _____

   _____

10. if
   _____

   _____

Find the Words–Level A

Directions: There are 10 Instant Words hidden here. Can you find and circle them?

Here are the words to look for:

do, how, she, there, which, an, each, if, their, use

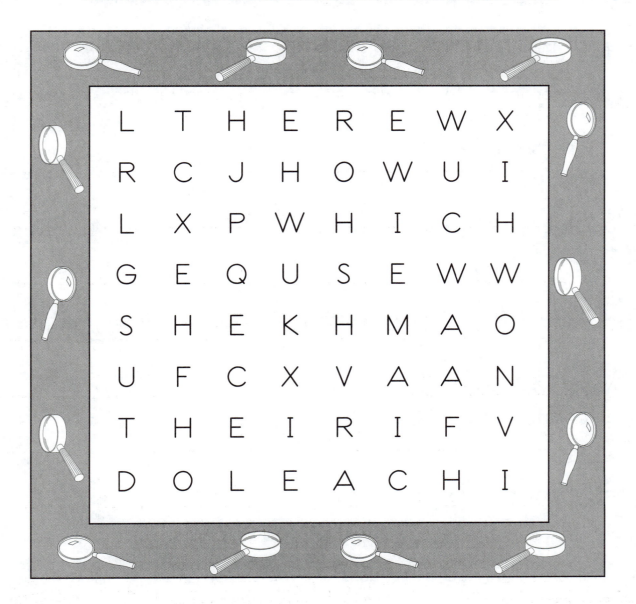

```
L T H E R E W X
R C J H O W U I
L X P W H I C H
G E Q U S E W W
S H E K H M A O
U F C X V A A N
T H E I R I F V
D O L E A C H I
```

Match Sentences with Pictures

Directions: Draw a line from each sentence to the picture it describes.

| use, an, each, which, she, there, do, how, their, if |

boy   elephant   fork   spoon   pencil   giraffe   monkey   chair

1. There is an elephant with a monkey.   a.

2. Each boy can have a pencil.   b.

3. Is that their giraffe?

c.

4. What do you do if you have an elephant on your chair?   d.

5. How can an elephant use a fork?   e.

6. Which spoon can she use?   f.

64

Name _____
Unit 5

Find the Words—Level B

Directions: There are 10 Instant Words hidden here. Can you find and circle them?

Here are the words to look for:

an, each, if, their, use, do, how, she, there, which

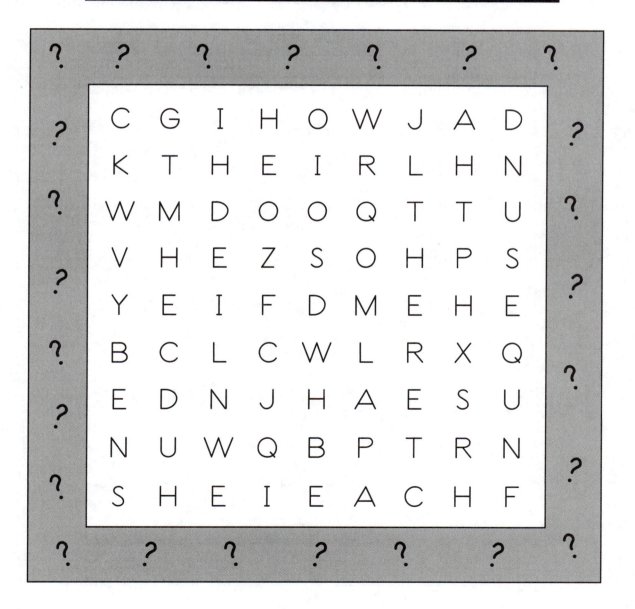

Unit 5

Choose the Correct Words

Directions: Choose the correct word to complete each sentence and write the word in the space.

| there, use, an, each, which, she, do, how, their, if |

boy   girl   elephant   pencil

1   The boy and girl are with _____ elephant.
                                              there their

2.   _____ pencil can you use?
                                Which How

3.   _____ can use that pencil.
                                If She

4.      _____ girl is by an elephant.
                                If Each

5.   An elephant can not _____ that.
                                                do each

6.      _____ can he be there?
                                There How

Just-for-Fun Letter Squares

Directions: Write the missing letters in the squares to spell the words from the word box. Then copy the completed words on the lines below the squares.

there, use, an, each, which, she, do, how, their, if

1. [t] [h] [ ] [i] [ ]

6. [e] [ ] [ ] [ ]

2. [s] [ ] [ ]

7. [ ] [s] [ ]

3. [ ] [n]

8. [d] [ ]

4. [ ] [ ] [i] [c] [h]

9. [ ] [f]

5. [t] [h] [ ] [r] [ ]

10. [h] [ ] [ ]

Flashcards

Directions: Cut out the flashcards and use them to help you learn the words.

will, up, other, about, out, many, then, them, these, so

will	many
up	then
other	them
about	these
out	so

Name _____

Write the Words

Directions: Write the words in the spaces.

will, up, other, about, out, many, then, them, these, so

1. will _____

   will
   _____

2. up _____

   _____

3. other _____

   _____

4. about _____

   _____

5. out _____

   _____

6. many _____

   _____

7. then _____

   _____

8. them _____

   _____

9. these _____

   _____

10. so _____

    _____

Find the Words—Level A

Directions: There are 10 Instant Words hidden here. Can you find and circle them?

Here are the words to look for:

about, other, so, then, up, many, out, them, these, will

U P Y R M R S O
E J C A T H E M
H N P Y J L U O
P O T H E R C N
L E A B O U T E
U D J T H E S E
M A N Y T H E N
W I L L O U T N

Name _____  Unit 6

Match Sentences with Pictures

Directions: Draw a line from each sentence to the picture it describes.

will, up, about, out, these, other, many, then, them, so

climb   boy   chicken   bear   mountain   tree   girl

1. The bear will climb up the mountain.   a.

2. Which tree will the other girl climb?   b.

3. So many of them are on the mountain.   c.

4. Then the boy will climb out of the tree.   d.

5 These chickens cannot climb up the tree.   e.

6. The boy is about to go up the tree.   f.

Find the Words—Level B

Directions: There are 10 Instant Words hidden here. Can you find and circle them?

Here are the words to look for:

about, other, so, then, up, many, out, them, these, will

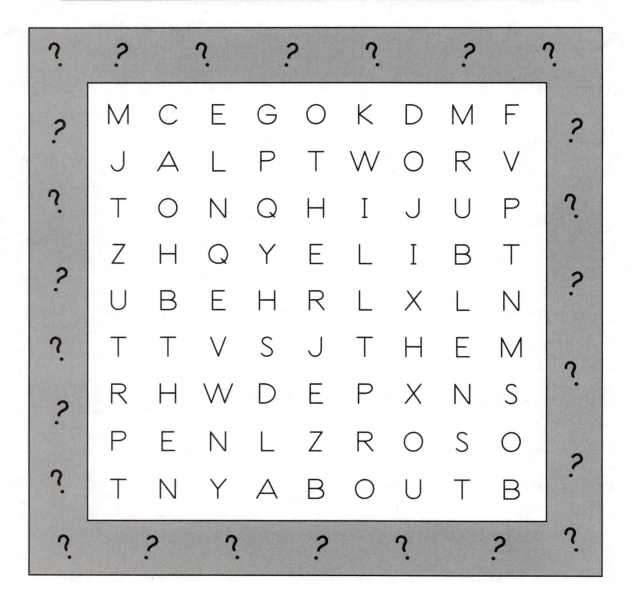

Name _____

Choose the Correct Words

Directions: Choose the correct word to complete each sentence and write the word in the space.

will, up, other, about, out, many, then, them, these, so

climb   girl   bear   book   mountain   tree

1. This book is _____ a bear.
   other about

2. _____ cats will not climb out of the tree.
   These Then

3. The bear is by _____ .
   then them

4. _____ of them were up in that tree.
   Many These

5. She will climb up the mountain and _____ will the other girl.
   so up

6. Will the _____ bear climb up in the tree?
   about other

Name _____

Just-for-Fun Word Scramble

Directions: Unscramble the mixed-up words below. Write the correct word from the word box on each line.

will, up, other, about, out, many, then, them, these, so

1. aymn _____

2. os _____

3. rhoet _____

4. liwl _____

5. uto _____

6. ehmt _____

7. taubo _____

8. neht _____

9. pu _____

10. eshte _____

Name _____  Unit 7

Flashcards

Directions: Cut out the flashcards and use them to help you learn the words.

some, her, would, make, like, him, into, time, has, look

some	him
her	into
would	time
make	has
like	look

Name _____  Unit 7

Write the Words

Directions: Write the words in the spaces.

some, her, would, make, like, him, into, time, has, look

1. some _____

    some _____

2. her _____

3. would _____

4. make _____

5. like _____

6. him _____

7. into _____

8. time _____

9. has _____

10. look _____

Unit 7

Find the Words–Level A

Directions: There are 10 Instant Words hidden here. Can you find and circle them?

Here are the words to look for:

has, him, like, make, time, her, into, look, some, would

Match Sentences with Pictures

Directions: Draw a line from each sentence to the picture it describes.

her, like, him, time, look, some, would, make, into, has

rabbit   tiger   book   picture   fish

1. He would like more time to look at the book about a rabbit.

    a.

2. The tiger was into the fish.

    b.

3. She would like to make the picture for him.

    c.

4. She has a rabbit with her.

    d.

5. She has some fish.

    e.

6. What time can you be there?

    f.

Name _____  Unit 7

Find the Words—Level B

Directions: There are 10 Instant Words hidden here. Can you find and circle them?

Here are the words to look for:

has, him, like, make, time, her, into, look, some, would

```
H  E  R  D  E  H  S  I  B
C  L  N  P  S  Q  O  T  R
J  S  L  O  O  K  M  I  T
O  V  I  W  M  F  X  M  Z
W  Y  K  P  E  R  J  E  E
W  O  E  M  A  I  N  T  O
H  O  U  X  M  A  K  E  I
U  I  K  L  C  F  H  A  S
B  R  M  S  D  Q  U  G  M
```

Choose the Correct Words

Directions: Choose the correct word to complete each sentence and write the word in the space.

some, her, would, make, like, him, into, time, has, look

fish   rabbit   tiger   book   picture

1. He has time to _____ at the other book.

like   look

2.  She will make a picture of _____ fish.

into   some

3.  _____ you like to have this rabbit?

Would   Make

4.  The picture is of _____ .

her   him

5.  She _____ a picture of a tiger on her book.

has   time

6.  We have _____ to make one other picture.

time   into

Name _____

Just-for-Fun Missing Letters

Directions: The words on the popcorn bags are each missing a letter. Fill in the missing letters to spell the words from the word box. Then copy the completed words on the lines below the popcorn bags.

some, her, would, make, like, him, into, time, has, look

1. wou___d

2. lik___

3. lo___k

4. som___

5. h___m

6. tim___

7. h___r

8. int___

9. mak___

10. ha___

Flashcards

Directions: Cut out the flashcards and use them to help you learn the words.

two, more, write, go, see, number, no, way, could, people

two	number
more	no
write	way
go	could
see	people

Name _____  Unit 8

Write the Words

Directions: Write the words in the spaces.

| two, more, write, go, see, number, no, way, could, people |

1. two
   _____
   _____two_____
   _____

2. more
   _____
   _____

3. write
   _____
   _____

4. go
   _____
   _____

5. see
   _____
   _____

6. number
   _____
   _____

7. no
   _____
   _____

8. way
   _____
   _____

9. could
   _____
   _____

10. people
    _____
    _____

Name _____

Unit 8

Find the Words—Level A

Directions: There are 10 Instant Words hidden here. Can you find and circle them?

Here are the words to look for:

could, more, number, see, way, go, no, people, two, write

```
T W O J O W A Y F
H N U M B E R A Q
H P E O P L E G O
K K O F L L C V R
N O F C W S T E L
N U R J D S E E U
C W I N N X L R G
Y K X W R I T E D
M O R E C O U L D
```

84

Name _____

Match Sentences with Pictures

Directions: Draw a line from each sentence to the picture it describes.

write, go, see, number, people, two, more, no, way, could

man   children   plane   school   book   men   picture

1. Two more men will be on the plane.   a.

2. A number of people were at the school.   b.

3. No, the man will not write a book for the rabbit, but he will write one for children.   c.

4. These children can go to see the plane.   d.

5. Could you make a picture for them?   e.

6. Which way do I go to see the plane?   f.

Find the Words–Level B

Directions: There are 10 Instant Words hidden here. Can you find and circle them?

Here are the words to look for:

> could, more, number, see, way, go, no, people, two, write

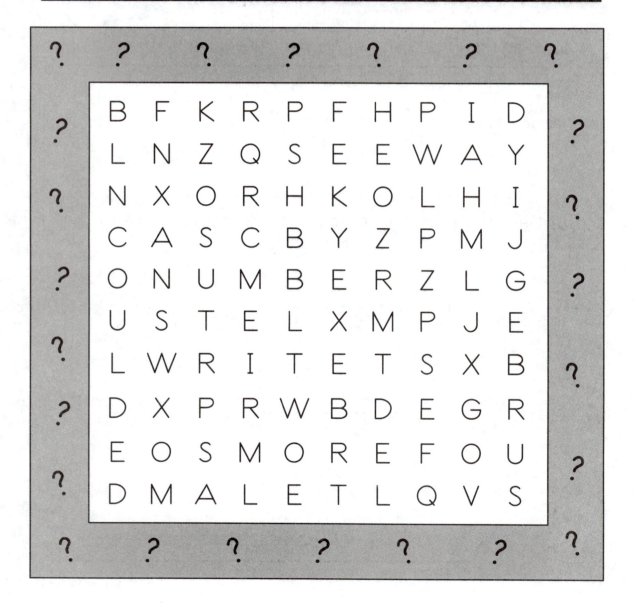

```
B F K R P F H P I D
L N Z Q S E E W A Y
N X O R H K O L H I
C A S C B Y Z P M J
O N U M B E R Z L G
U S T E L X M P J E
L W R I T E T S X B
D X P R W B D E G R
E O S M O R E F O U
D M A L E T L Q V S
```

Choose the Correct Words

Directions: Choose the correct word to complete each sentence and write the word in the space.

two, more, write, go, see, number, no, way, could, people

man   children   plane   book

1. The two children will _____ a book.
   number write

2. Two _____ people were at the plane.
   more could

3. There is no _____ he can go on that.
   way more

4. A _____ of people were on the plane.
   could number

5. The children will _____ to see a
   man write a book.   no go

6. We will go _____ the plane when it is
   not in the air.   see way

Name _____

Unit 8

Just-for-Fun Spelling

Directions: Cut apart the letters on this page. Use the letters to spell each of the words in the word box.

two, more, write, go, see, number, no, way, could, people

a	b	c	d	e
e	g	i	l	m
n	o	p	r	s
t	u	w	y	p

Flashcards

Directions: Cut out the flashcards and use them to help you learn the words.

my, than, first, water, been, call, who, oil, now, find

my	call
than	who
first	oil
water	now
been	find

Name _____  Unit 9

Write the Words

Directions: Write the words in the spaces.

| my, than, first, water, been, call, who, oil, now, find |

1. my _____

   _____ *my* _____

2. than _____

   _____

3. first _____

   _____

4. water _____

   _____

5. been _____

   _____

6. call _____

   _____

7. who _____

   _____

8. oil _____

   _____

9. now _____

   _____

10. find _____

   _____

Unit 9

Find the Words—Level A

Directions: There are 10 Instant Words hidden here. Can you find and circle them?

Here are the words to look for:

been, find, my, oil, water, call, first, now, than, who

Match Sentences with Pictures

Directions: Draw a line from each sentence to the picture it describes.

first, water, call, oil, find, my, than, been, who, now

drink

boy

girl

school

1. The boy will be first to drink the water.   a.

2. We can find oil if we look.   b.

3. The girl has been at school all this time.   c.

4. Now who can that be?   d.

5. He will be the first to call my number.   e.

6. There were more people than I could see.   f.

Name _____

Unit 9

Find the Words—Level B

Directions: There are 10 Instant Words hidden here. Can you find and circle them?

Here are the words to look for:

been, find, my, oil, water, call, first, now, than, who

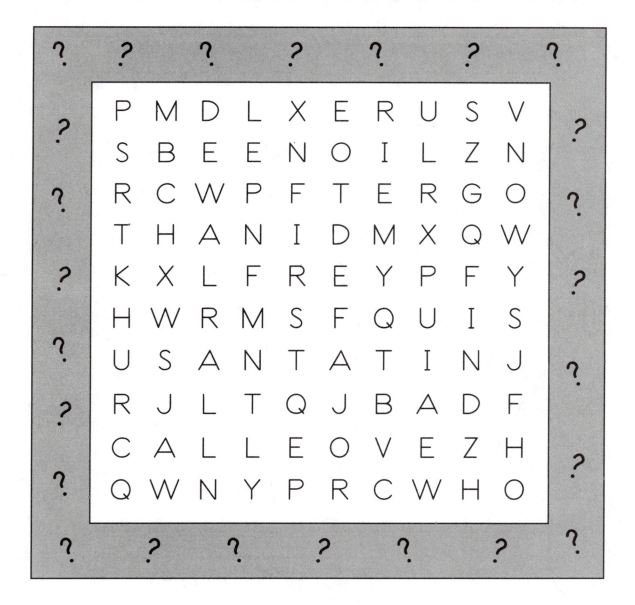

P M D L X E R U S V
S B E E N O I L Z N
R C W P F T E R G O
T H A N I D M X Q W
K X L F R E Y P F Y
H W R M S F Q U I S
U S A N T A T I N J
R J L T Q J B A D F
C A L L E O V E Z H
Q W N Y P R C W H O

Unit 9

Choose the Correct Words

Directions: Choose the correct word to complete each sentence and write the word in the space.

my, than, first, water, been, call, who, oil, now, find

1. Who will be the _____ to call?
   <u>first find</u>

2. _____ dog can drink that water.
   <u>Been My</u>

3. They will look for _____ .
   <u>oil than</u>

4. His dog has _____ in the water.
   <u>now been</u>

5. She cannot _____ him now.
   <u>now find</u>

6. _____ will call you?
   <u>Who Than</u>

Just-for-Fun Mystery Words

Be a detective! Can you use the code symbols to solve the mystery words?

Directions: Look at the code symbols under each line. Match each symbol to each letter and fill in the letters on each line. Check the words that you made to make sure they match the instant words in the box.

my, than, first, water, been, call, who, oil, now, find

1. __ __ __ __
   ↑ ✳ ☆ ☆

2. __ __ __ __
   ⊠ ⊙ ✳ →

3. __ __ __ __ __
   ◬ ✳ ⊠ □ ■

4. __ __ __
   ◬ ⊙ ●

5. __ __
   ♥ ★

6. __ __ __ __
   ↓ ✕ → ÷

7. __ __ __ __ __
   ↓ ✕ ■ ♡ ⊠

8. __ __ __
   ● ✕ ☆

9. __ __ __
   → ● ◬

10. __ __ __ __
   △ □ □ →

Code Symbols

a = ✳   b = △   c = ↑   d = ÷   e = □   f = ↓   g = ▼   h = ⊙   i = ✕

j = ○   k = ▽   l = ☆   m = ♥   n = →   o = ●   p = ⊡   q = ←   r = ■

s = ♡   t = ⊠   u = ▲   v = +   w = ◬   x = ✲   y = ★   z = ⊗

Flashcards

Directions: Cut out the flashcards and use them to help you learn the words.

long, down, day, did, get, come, made, may, part, over

long	come
down	made
day	may
did	part
get	over

Write the Words

Directions: Write the words in the spaces.

long, down, day, did, get, come, made, may, part, over

1. long _____

   _____ long _____

2. down _____

   _____

3. day _____

   _____

4. did _____

   _____

5. get _____

6. come _____

   _____

7. made _____

   _____

8. may _____

   _____

9. part _____

   _____

10. over _____

   _____

Name _____  Unit 10

Find the Words—Level A

Directions: There are 10 Instant Words hidden here. Can you find and circle them?

Here are the words to look for:

come, did, long, may, own, day, get, made, over, part

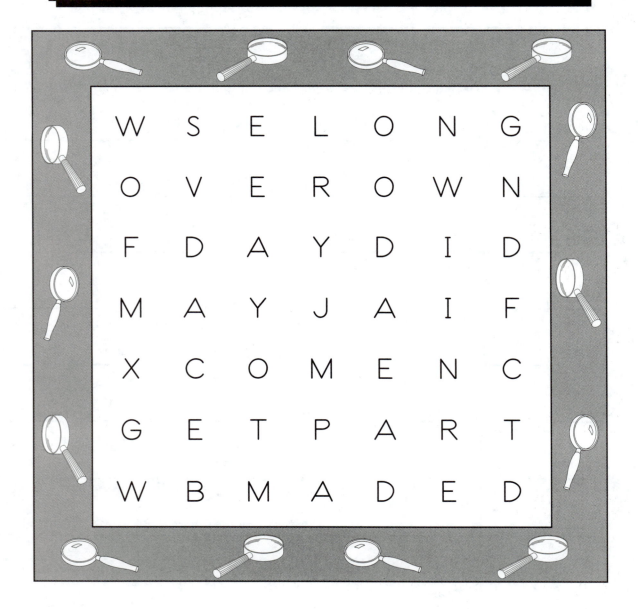

```
W  S  E  L  O  N  G
O  V  E  R  O  W  N
F  D  A  Y  D  I  D
M  A  Y  J  A  I  F
X  C  O  M  E  N  C
G  E  T  P  A  R  T
W  B  M  A  D  E  D
```

Name _____

Match Sentences with Pictures

Directions: Draw a line from each sentence to the picture it describes.

long, down, day, part, over, did, get, come, made, may

eye   face   feet   hand   head   sun   dog   book picture

1. She has her hand over her head. a.

2. How did you get your dog to come with you? b.

3. He has his hand down on his long feet. c. 

4. She made a picture of part of the sun. d.

5. Your eye is part of your face. e.

6. May I look at your book one day? f.

Find the Words–Level B

Directions: There are 10 Instant Words hidden here. Can you find and circle them?

Here are the words to look for:

| come, did, long, may, down, day, get, made, over, part |

```
?     ?     ?      ?      ?      ?       ?
  P  B  A  S  T  R  M  N  B  N
? A  C  D  M  P  G  E  T  O  Q  ?
? R  O  J  B  A  I  J  E  V  U  ?
  T  U  E  L  D  D  S  P  E  R
? B  D  S  B  O  O  E  Q  R  Z  ?
  N  I  Z  A  W  N  X  I  E  Y
? T  D  E  R  N  R  G  J  D  S  ?
? X  B  O  N  P  R  B  V  A  T
  M  C  O  M  E  S  M  A  Y  M  ?
? U  T  S  E  Y  V  S  J  D  N
?     ?     ?      ?      ?      ?       ?
```

Choose the Correct Words

Directions: Choose the correct word to complete each sentence and write the word in the space.

long, down, day, did, get, come, made, may, part, over

picture   dog

1. What _____ you get from her?
   day did

2. He made a picture of a _____ dog.
   long part

3. Can you come _____ some day?
   over may

4. Come _____ from there!
   made down

5. What day did you _____ that from him?
   get part

6. His dog can go _____ that.
   may over

Just-for-Fun Letter Squares

Directions: Write the missing letters in the squares to spell the words from the word box. Then copy the completed words on the lines below the squares.

long, down, day, did, get, come, made, may, part, over

1. ☐ i ☐

_____

2. m ☐ ☐ e

_____

3. ☐ ☐ ☐ g

_____

4. d ☐ ☐ n

_____

5. d a ☐

_____

6. m ☐ ☐

_____

7. o ☐ ☐ ☐

_____

8. ☐ e ☐

_____

9. p ☐ ☐ ☐

_____

10. c ☐ ☐ ☐

_____

Name _____  Unit 11

Flashcards

Directions: Cut out the flashcards and use them to help you learn the words.

new, sound, take, only, little, work, know, place, year, live

new	work
sound	know
take	place
only	year
little	live

Name _____

Write the Words

Directions: Write the words in the spaces.

new, sound, take, only, little, work, know, place, year, live

1. new _____

2. sound _____

3. take _____

4. only _____

5. little _____

6. work _____

7. know _____

8. place _____

9. year _____

10. live _____

Name _____

Find the Words—Level A

Directions: There are 10 Instant Words hidden here. Can you find and circle them?

Here are the words to look for:

know, live, only, sound, work, little, new, place, take, year

```
O N L Y I T A K E
N E W L I V E P I
Y Q U P K N O W W
D I P E N F D C D
U S O U N D A S N
N P L A C E H S I
W O R K Y E A R T
H L V W L G J C S
W H L I T T L E X
```

Name _____

Match Pictures with Sentences

Directions: Circle **a** or **b** to choose the sentence that best describes each picture.

little, work, know, place, year, new, sound, take, only, live

rabbit   desk   school

1.
    a. School is the place I work.
    b. School is the place other people get oil.

2.
    a. She will live in this little place.
    b. She will go to school this year.

3.
    a. I made my desk at school.
    b. I work at my desk at school.

4.
    a. I know what year it is.
    b. I know how to do my work.

5.
    a. The people made a new sound.
    b. She will only take two.

6.
    a. Do you know which one is for the rabbit?
    b. These are all new.

Find the Words—Level B

Directions: There are 10 Instant Words hidden here. Can you find and circle them?

Here are the words to look for:

know, live, only, sound, work, little, new, place, take, year

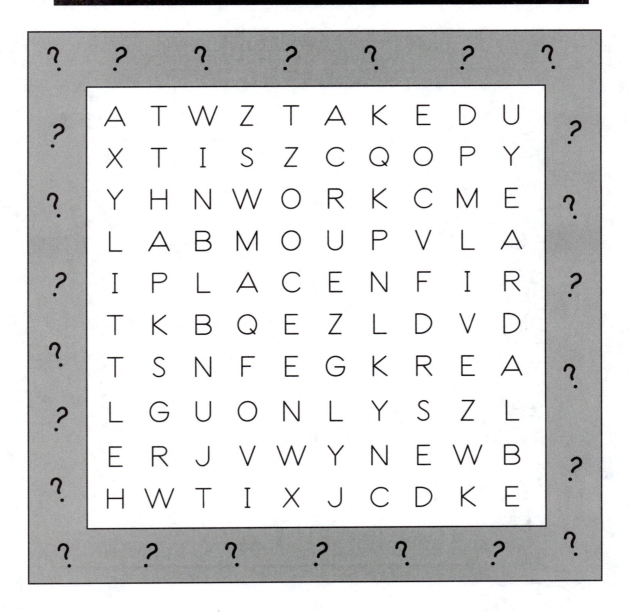

Name _____

Choose the Correct Words

Directions: Choose the correct word to complete each sentence and write the word in the space.

new, sound, take, only, little, work, know, place, year, live

rabbit   desk

1. Can you _____ this to him?
   only take

2. What was that new _____ ?
   place sound

3. I do not _____ what it is.
   know work

4. My desk is _____ this year.
   new only

5. What will _____ in this?
   year live

6. A little rabbit can get in this _____ place.
   little work

108

Just-for-Fun Word Scramble

Directions: Unscramble the mixed-up words below. Write the correct word from the word box on each line.

new, sound, take, only, little, work, know, place, year, live

1. keta _____

2. kwor _____

3. lepca _____

4. enw _____

5. lyno _____

6. eilv _____

7. nusod _____

8. tiltel _____

9. arye _____

10. owkn _____

Unit 12

Flashcards

Directions: Cut out the flashcards and use them to help you learn the words.

me, back, give, most, very, after, thing, our, just, name

me	after
back	thing
give	our
most	just
very	name

Name _____

Write the Words

Directions: Write the words in the spaces.

me, back, give, most, very, after, thing, our, just, name

1. me _____

2. back _____

3. give _____

4. most _____

5. very _____

6. after _____

7. thing _____

8. our _____

9. just _____

10. name _____

Name _____  Unit 12

Find the Words—Level A

Directions: There are 10 Instant Words hidden here. Can you find and circle them?

Here are the words to look for:

> after, give, me, name, thing, back, just, most, our, very

```
B E Y W A S V Z
T X U P H O M U
O U R T H I N G
B A C K G I V E
K A F T E R M E
T I M O S T S V
J U S T N A M E
X V E R Y E N W
```

Match Pictures with Sentences

Directions: Circle **a** or **b** to choose the sentence that best describes each picture.

back, give, thing, our, name, me, most, very, after, just

fly   dog   house

1. a. This is in back of our house.
   b. My house is after me!

2. a. This thing can live in your house.
   b. This thing will fly by my house.

3. a. Write your name on this.
   b. What is the name of that dog?

4. a. This is just a little thing.
   b. This is not very little.

5. a. Our name is on our house.
   b. Give this to your dog.

6. a. I can get to work just in time.
   b. I know most people fly these.

Find the Words—Level B

Directions: There are 10 Instant Words hidden here. Can you find and circle them?

Here are the words to look for:

after, give, me, name, thing, back, just, most, our, very

```
? ? ? ? ? ? ?
?  A U N J K L E S F A  ?
   C T P A O B A C K H
?  V H B W M V G M K V  ?
   L I T J D E F J Q E
?  W N C G N X M U G R  ?
   D G Q R I Z E S I Y
?  K X M J D V Y T H U  ?
   Y M O S T Z E G I P
?  F A F T E R I O U R  ?
   R Z B H C S N T O B
? ? ? ? ? ? ?
```

Choose the Correct Words

Directions: Choose the correct word to complete each sentence and write the word in the space.

me, back, give, most, very, after, thing, our, just, name

1. I can do my work _____ I do this.
   very   after

2.  I like you the _____ .
   most   just

3. That thing is not _____ long.
   very   me

4. I will write my _____ .
   back   name

5. Will you _____ this to her for me?
   thing   give

6. _____ name is on it.
   Just   Our

Just-for-Fun Missing Letters

Directions: The words on the basketballs are each missing a letter. Fill in the missing letters to spell the words from the word box. Then copy the completed words on the lines below the basketballs.

me, back, give, most, very, after, thing, our, just, name

3. thi _ g

_____

1. ba _ k

_____

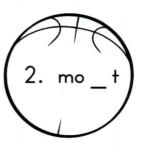
2. mo _ t

_____

4. m _

_____

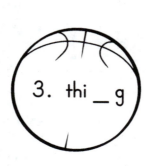
5. o _ r

_____

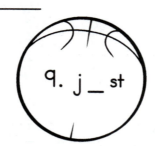
6. nam _

_____

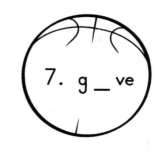
7. g _ ve

_____

8. aft _ r

_____

9. j _ st

_____

10. ver _

_____

Name _____

Flashcards

Directions: Cut out the flashcards and use them to help you learn the words.

good, sentence, man, think, say, great, where, help, through, much

good	great
sentence	where
man	help
think	through
say	much

Write the Words

Directions: Write the words in the spaces.

good, sentence, man, think, say, great, where, help, through, much

1. good _____

2. sentence _____

3. man _____

4. think _____

5. say _____

6. great _____

7. where _____

8. help _____

9. through _____

10. much _____

Name _____

Find the Words—Level A

Directions: There are 10 Instant Words hidden here. Can you find and circle them?

Here are the words to look for:

good, help, much, sentence, through, great, man, say, think, where

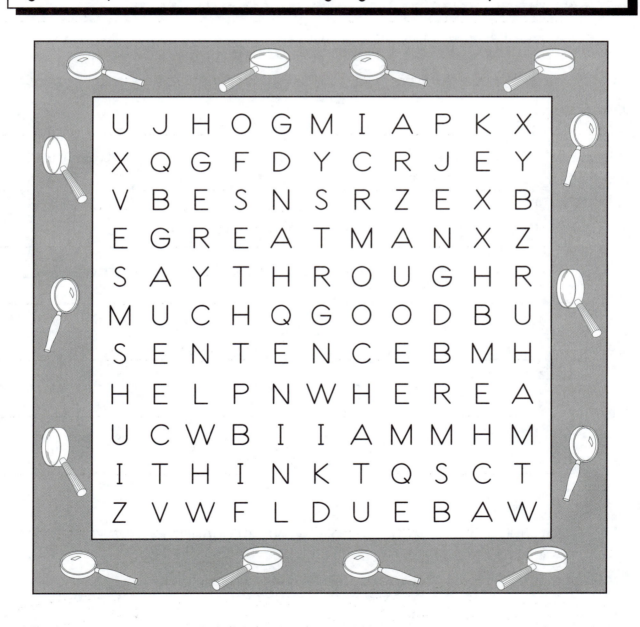

```
U  J  H  O  G  M  I  A  P  K  X
X  Q  G  F  D  Y  C  R  J  E  Y
V  B  E  S  N  S  R  Z  E  X  B
E  G  R  E  A  T  M  A  N  X  Z
S  A  Y  T  H  R  O  U  G  H  R
M  U  C  H  Q  G  O  O  D  B  U
S  E  N  T  E  N  C  E  B  M  H
H  E  L  P  N  W  H  E  R  E  A
U  C  W  B  I  I  A  M  M  H  M
I  T  H  I  N  K  T  Q  S  C  T
Z  V  W  F  L  D  U  E  B  A  W
```

Name _____

Match Pictures with Sentences

Directions: Circle **a** or **b** to choose the sentence that best describes each picture.

good, sentence, think, where, help, man, say, great, through, much

custodian   teacher

1.
   a. The teacher said, "That is a good sentence."
   b. Where did they go on that day?

2.
   a. I do not think I know you.
   b. The custodian can help you with that.

3.
   a. We will have a great time.
   b. What did that man say?

4.
   a. It is a great day to do this.
   b. It just went through there.

5.
   a. How much is it?
   b. The people went through it.

6.
   a. Where were they then?
   b. You have been very good.

Name _____  Unit 13

Find the Words—Level B

Directions: There are 10 Instant Words hidden here. Can you find and circle them?

Here are the words to look for:

| great, man, say, think, where, good, help, much, sentence, through |

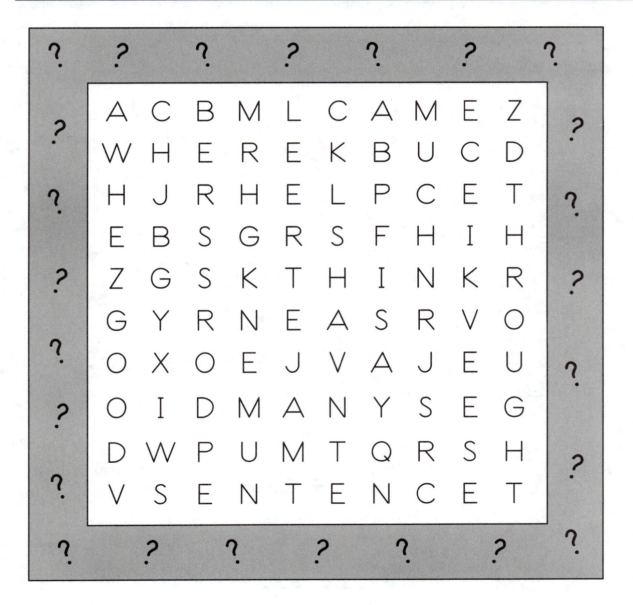

Name _____ Unit 13

Choose the Correct Words

Directions: Choose the correct word to complete each sentence and write the word in the space.

> good, sentence, man, think, say, great, where, help, through, much

1.  _____ did they all go?
   Where Help

2.  Are you all _____ with your work?
   think through

3.  I made a good _____ just now.
   great sentence

4.  How _____ can we give to them?
   much man

5. That is a _____ thing for you to do.
   through great

6. Did she _____ that you could come over?
   say good

Just-for-Fun Spelling

Directions: Cut apart the letters on this page. Use the letters to spell each of the words in the word box.

good, sentence, man, think, say, great, where, help, through, much

a	c	d	e	e	e
g	h	i	k	l	m
n	n	o	o	p	r
s	t	u	w	y	h

Flashcards

Directions: Cut out the flashcards and use them to help you learn the words.

before, line, right, too, mean, old, any, same, tell, boy

before	old
line	any
right	same
too	tell
mean	boy

Name _____  Unit 14

Write the Words

Directions: Write the words in the spaces.

before, line, right, too, mean, old, any, same, tell, boy

1. before _____

2. line _____

3. right _____

4. too _____

5. mean _____

6. old _____

7. any _____

8. same _____

9. tell _____

10. boy _____

Name _____

Unit 14

Find the Words—Level A

Directions: There are 10 Instant Words hidden here. Can you find and circle them?

Here are the words to look for:

before, line, old, same, too, any, boy, mean, right, tell

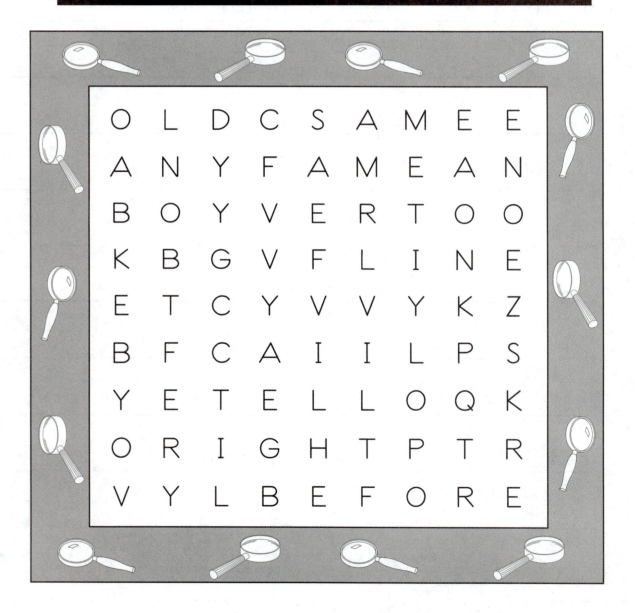

O L D C S A M E E
A N Y F A M E A N
B O Y V E R T O O
K B G V F L I N E
E T C Y V V Y K Z
B F C A I I L P S
Y E T E L L O Q K
O R I G H T P T R
V Y L B E F O R E

Match Pictures with Sentences

Directions: Circle **a** or **b** to choose the sentence that best describes each picture.

line, too, old, tell, boy, before, right, mean, any, same

girl   school

1.
   a. The girl is in back of the boy in line.
   b. The old man will help them.

2.
   a. Tell me how to write my name.
   b. It is too old to use now.

3.
   a. I do this before I go to school.
   b. We are right on time.

4.
   a. I will be there at the same time as before.
   b. What did they mean by that?

5.
   a. We can use any that you have.
   b. He is very mean.

6.
   a. Is this the same person?
   b. You are right about that.

Name _____

Find the Words—Level B

Directions: There are 10 Instant Words hidden here. Can you find and circle them?

Here are the words to look for:

any, boy, mean, right, tell, before, line, old, same, too

```
? ? ? ? ? ? ?
?   O L S L O W X C Y I   ?
    O T B R I B J M J S
?   L B D O E N H E R A   ?
    D F A N Y V E A R M
?   G W E T U G E N S E   ?
    V M R I G H T S T Z
?   N A D C U B E D E K   ?
?   B E F O R E Q E L S
    H I E B T O O I L L   ?
?   J Q K F E P T X A T
? ? ? ? ? ? ?
```

Name ____________________ Unit 14

Choose the Correct Words

Directions: Choose the correct word to complete each sentence and write the word in the space.

before, line, right, too, mean, old, any, same, tell, boy

1. 

Have some of these __________ you go.
same before

2. 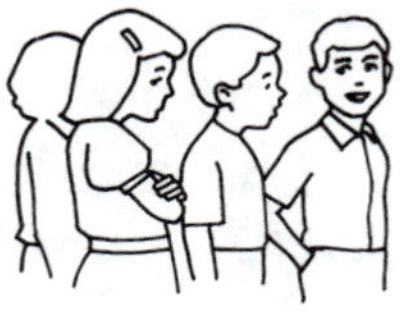

Do you think this is the __________ line?
right before

3. 

They have the __________ name.
same any

4. 

She is __________ little.
old too

5. 

The boy did not __________ to do that.
mean boy

6. 

This is too __________ .
tell old

Unit 14

Just-for-Fun Mystery Words

Be a detective! Can you use the code symbols to solve the mystery words?

Directions: Look at the code symbols under each line. Match each symbol to each letter and fill in the letters on each line. Check the words that you made to make sure they match the instant words in the box.

before, line, right, too, mean, old, any, same, tell, boy

1. ___ ___ ___
   △   ●   ★

2. ___ ___ ___ ___
   ♡   ✳   ♥   □

3. ___ ___ ___
   ⊠   ●   ●

4. ___ ___ ___ ___ ___ ___
   △   □   ↓   ●   ■   □

5. ___ ___ ___
   ●   ☆   ÷

6. ___ ___ ___ ___
   ⊠   □   ☆   ☆

7. ___ ___ ___ ___
   ♥   □   ✳   →

8. ___ ___ ___
   ✳   →   ★

9. ___ ___ ___ ___ ___
   ■   ✕   ▼   ⊙   ⊠

10. ___ ___ ___ ___
    ☆   ✕   →   □

Code Symbols

a = ✳ b = △ c = ↑ d = ÷ e = □ f = ↓ g = ▼ h = ⊙ i = ✕
j = ○ k = ▽ l = ☆ m = ♥ n = → o = ● p = ⊡ q = ← r = ■
s = ♡ t = ⊠ u = ▲ v = + w = ◭ x = ✿ y = ★ z = ⊗

Flashcards

Directions: Cut out the flashcards and use them to help you learn the words.

follow, came, want, show, also, around, form, three, small, set

follow	around
came	form
want	three
show	small
also	set

Name _____  Unit 15

Write the Words

Directions: Write the words in the spaces.

> follow, came, want, show, also, around, form, three, small, set

1. follow _____

2. came _____

3. want _____

4. show _____

5. also _____

6. around _____

7. form _____

8. three _____

9. small _____

10. set _____

Name _____  Unit 15

Find the Words—Level A

Directions: There are 10 Instant Words hidden here. Can you find and circle them?

Here are the words to look for:

| also, came, form, show, three, around, follow, set, small, want |

```
S  E  T  C  A  M  E  B  B
P  S  H  O  W  G  S  Q  X
A  R  O  U  N  D  X  V  X
T  H  R  E  E  A  L  S  O
L  S  M  A  L  L  A  L  A
A  F  O  R  M  H  Z  R  T
M  X  T  K  I  W  P  N  M
U  I  G  F  O  L  L  O  W
I  W  V  N  W  A  N  T  H
```

Match Pictures with Sentences

Directions: Circle **a** or **b** to choose the sentence that best describes each picture.

came, show, form, three, small, follow, want, also, around, set

teacher   bus driver   secretary   principal   custodian   draw

1.   a. The teacher will show you where it is.
     b. The teacher will help him form the number three.

2.   a. The secretary will show you what you need.
     b. She came to the show with them.

3.   a. The principal will help the small boy.
     b. The principal will help the bus driver.

4.   a. Did you follow what I said?
     b. All of these people also live there.

5.   a. The custodian will set that down.
     b. They will set that down right there.

6.   a. I want to draw on that.
     b. They will follow her around.

Unit 15

Find the Words–Level B

Directions: There are 10 Instant Words hidden here. Can you find and circle them?

Here are the words to look for:

also, came, form, show, three, around, follow, set, small, want

```
?    ?    ?    ?    ?    ?    ?

?   R  E  W  A  N  T  I  S  A  N    ?
    S  E  S  T  F  E  H  J  U  P
?   E  V  C  E  O  P  U  R  A  R    ?
    T  O  R  A  R  I  S  R  E  I
?   E  M  E  N  M  O  H  O  T  E    ?
    A  E  J  Q  X  E  O  I  S  M
?   A  L  E  S  T  O  W  P  U  Q    ?
?   J  O  S  A  R  O  U  N  D  U
    E  E  F  O  L  L  O  W  E  R    ?
?   T  S  M  A  L  L  A  L  M  S

?    ?    ?    ?    ?    ?    ?
```

Choose the Correct Words

Directions: Choose the correct word to complete each sentence and write the word in the space.

follow, came, want, show, also, around, farm, three, small, set

teacher   bus driver   secretary   principal   custodian

1. Your teacher will _____ you how to do that.
   follow show

2. He may go _____ and around.
   around farm

3. Our principal _____ by to see the boy.
   came want

4. The bus driver will come by for all _____ of them.
   small three

5. She just got a new _____ of them.
   set also

6. The custodian will not want him to _____ you.
   around follow

Name _____

Unit 15

Just-for-Fun Letter Squares

Directions: Write the missing letters in the squares to spell the words from the word box. Then copy the completed words on the lines below the squares.

follow, came, want, show, also, around, farm, three, small, set

1. ☐f☐ ☐ ☐ ☐m☐

_____

2. ☐w☐ ☐ ☐ ☐

_____

3. ☐s☐ ☐h☐ ☐ ☐

_____

4. ☐t☐ ☐h☐ ☐ ☐ ☐

_____

5. ☐ ☐e☐ ☐

_____

6. ☐ ☐ ☐ ☐ ☐ ☐d☐

_____

7. ☐c☐ ☐ ☐ ☐

_____

8. ☐ ☐ ☐s☐ ☐o☐

_____

9. ☐s☐ ☐m☐ ☐ ☐ ☐

_____

10. ☐ ☐ ☐ ☐l☐ ☐l☐ ☐ ☐

_____

Flashcards

Directions: Cut out the flashcards and use them to help you learn the words.

put, end, does, another, well, large, must, big, even, such

put	large
end	must
does	big
another	even
well	such

138

Name _____

Write the Words

Directions: Write the words in the spaces.

| put, end, does, another, well, large, must, big, even, such |

1. put _____

2. end _____

3. does _____

4. another _____

5. well _____

6. large _____

7. must _____

8. big _____

9. even _____

10. such _____

Name _____

Find the Words—Level A

Directions: There are 10 Instant Words hidden here. Can you find and circle them?

Here are the words to look for:

another, does, even, must, such, big, end, large, put, well

140

Match Pictures with Sentences

Directions: Circle **a** or **b** to choose the sentence that best describes each picture.

put, another, large, big, such, end, does, well, must, even

shirt   pants   dress   shoes   hat

1.   a. He has large shoes.
   b. They all have such little shoes.

2.   a. She will put on another dress.
   b. She will put on another shirt.

3.   a. He will write another sentence about pants.
   b. He has on such a big hat.

4. 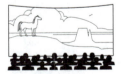   a. How do you think it will end?
   b. Does he know where you live?

5.   a. It is not even the right day.
   b. You must tell him when he does well.

6.   a. I will get even with him for that.
   b. I must call to see if he can come.

Name _____

Find the Words—Level B

Directions: There are 10 Instant Words hidden here. Can you find and circle them?

Here are the words to look for:

| another, does, even, must, such, big, end, large, put, well |

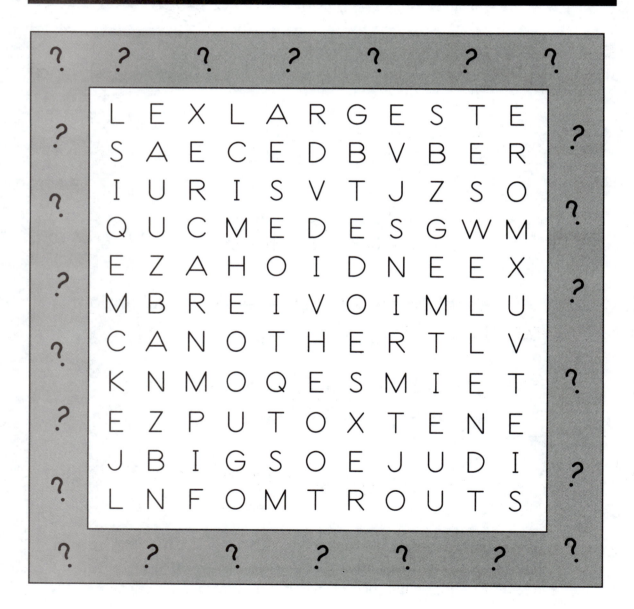

Unit 16

Choose the Correct Words

Directions: Choose the correct word to complete each sentence and write the word in the space.

put, end, does, another, well, large, must, big, even, such

shirt   pants   dress   shoes   hat

1. She cannot put on such a _____ dress.

   even large

2. He must get _____ hat.

   another does

3. You must not tell me how it will _____ .

   end well

4. You have on _____ a big shirt!

   large such

5. She _____ not want such big shoes.

   put does

6. You _____ be big before you can use these
   pants.   must big

Name _____

Just-for-Fun Word Scramble

Directions: Unscramble the mixed-up words below. Write the correct word from the word box on each line.

put, end, does, another, well, large, must, big, even, such

1. sutm _____

2. lewl _____

3. uhsc _____

4. oesd _____

5. nvee _____

6. henarot _____

7. gerla _____

8. utp _____

9. igb _____

10. nde _____

Flashcards

Directions: Cut out the flashcards and use them to help you learn the words.

because, turn, here, why, ask, went, men, read, need, land

because	went
turn	men
here	read
why	need
ask	land

Write the Words

Directions: Write the words in the spaces.

because, turn, here, why, ask, went, men, read, need, land

1. because _____

_____

2. turn _____

_____

3. here _____

_____

4. why _____

_____

5. ask _____

6. went _____

_____

7. men _____

_____

8. read _____

_____

9. need _____

_____

10. land _____

_____

Name _____  Unit 17

Find the Words—Level A

Directions: There are 10 Instant Words hidden here. Can you find and circle them?

Here are the words to look for:

ask, here, men, read, went, because, land, need, turn, why

```
D B E C A U S E R R
Y C T U R N E E D O
J O X N M E N C T O
H Y L A N D J D H L
R E F X Q M R O H G
I L K P D G C N P L
X P B E A S K T R S
T U Z N P A V Y L C
X W H Y N L H E R E
R E A D M W E N T F
```

Match Pictures with Sentences

Directions: Circle **a** or **b** to choose the sentence that best describes each picture.

turn, here, ask, read, need, because, why, went, men, land

pen   pencil   crayon   typewriter   computer

1. a. He went there to work.
    b. He is here because we are.

2. a. These two men can do this.
    b. These men live on old land.

3. a. Why did she write on that line?
    b. I do not know why she is there.

4. a. You can read what I write on this typewriter.
    b. It is her turn to follow the typewriter around.

5. a. Here is my new pen and pencil set.
    b. Here is my crayon.

6. a. Is it your turn to use the computer?
    b. I need to ask the computer for more water.

Find the Words—Level B

Directions: There are 10 Instant Words hidden here. Can you find and circle them?

Here are the words to look for:

> ask, here, men, read, went, because, land, need, turn, why

```
V E O J I W S T N P X
N Z N H E R E N I M E
A I J E Q O Z Q A Z D
E S B E C A U S E N R
Q U K L O P E N W H Y
P M E N X R U V S M E
S E R J O W E N T U T
A L A N D E R A R O U
S Z R T C A X K D D R
R E N E E D Z L Y S N
U X C O D M V J K L J
```

Name _____

Choose the Correct Words

Directions: Choose the correct word to complete each sentence and write the word in the space.

because, turn, here, why, ask, went, read, need, land, men

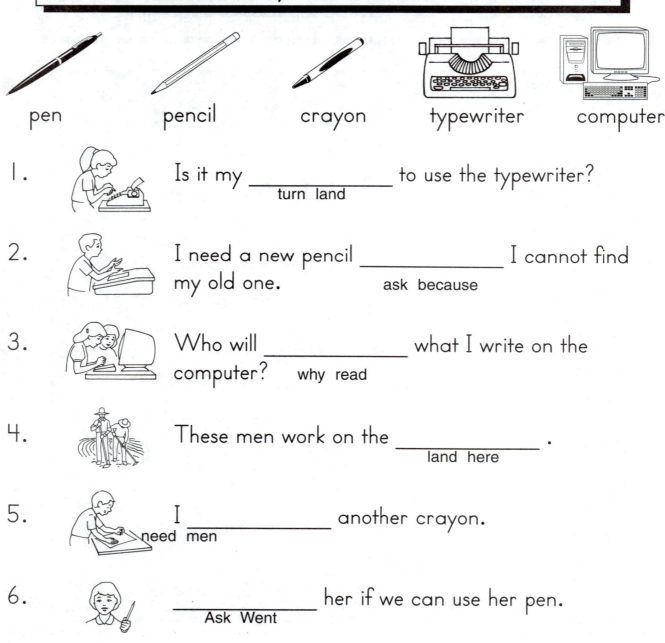

pen   pencil   crayon   typewriter   computer

1. Is it my _____ to use the typewriter?
    turn land

2. I need a new pencil _____ I cannot find
    my old one.   ask because

3. Who will _____ what I write on the
    computer?   why read

4. These men work on the _____ .
    land here

5. I _____ another crayon.
    need men

6. _____ her if we can use her pen.
    Ask Went

Just-for-Fun Missing Letters

Directions: The words on the kites are each missing a letter. Fill in the missing letters to spell the words from the word box. Then copy the completed words on the lines below the kites.

because, turn, here, why, ask, went, read, need, land, men

 1. re _ d

_____

 2. la _ d

_____

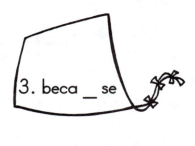 3. beca _ se

_____

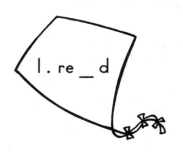 4. her _

_____

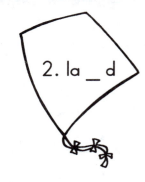 5. m _ n

_____

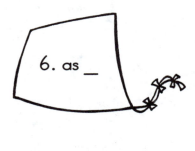 6. as _

_____

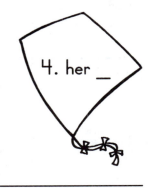 7. t _ rn

_____

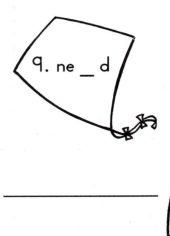 8. we _ t

_____

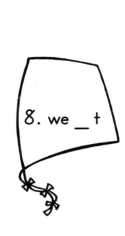 9. ne _ d

_____

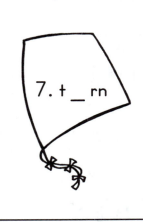 10. wh _

_____

Name _____

Flashcards

Directions: Cut out the flashcards and use them to help you learn the words.

different, home, us, move, try, kind, hand, picture, again, change

different	kind
home	hand
us	picture
move	again
try	change

Name _____

Write the Words

Directions: Write the words in the spaces.

> different, home, us, move, try, kind, hand, picture, again, change

1. different _____

_____

2. home _____

_____

3. us _____

_____

4. move _____

_____

5. try _____

_____

6. kind _____

_____

7. hand _____

_____

8. picture _____

_____

9. again _____

_____

10. change _____

_____

Find the Words—Level A

Directions: There are 10 Instant Words hidden here. Can you find and circle them?

Here are the words to look for:

| again, different, home, move, try, change, hand, kind, picture, us |

```
T E L V G B M O V E Q O
Q G Y T S I I P K I A O
O D I F F E R E N T L S
P I C T U R E T R Y Z N
W Y T F W L Y E T E K O
C X P R W M B J A Z W X
R R N V G I S B H K E A
S B M X C H A N G E U S
Q I W D D M W H O M E P
F E O A G A I N K I N D
J V D P Q H A N D O J R
O K Z L Y D H R H N N G
```

Name _____

Match Pictures with Sentences

Directions: Circle **a** or **b** to choose the sentence that best describes each picture.

home, move, try, hand, picture, different, us, kind, again, change

elephant   giraffe   bear   tiger   monkey   jump

1.   a. Will the tiger jump over it again?
   b. I live in a different place now.

2.   a. The bear is in his new home.
   b. The boy is very kind.

3.   a. We will move into our new home.
   b. We will move our home up and down.

4.   a. He will change that word to a different word.
   b. He will jump on that with us.

5.   a. This giraffe can jump.
   b. This monkey can use his hand like we do.

6.   a The monkey will take a picture of you.
   b. The elephant will try to get up on that.

Name _____ Unit 18

Find the Words–Level B

Directions: There are 10 Instant Words hidden here. Can you find and circle them?

Here are the words to look for:

| again, different, home, move, try, change, hand, kind, picture, us |

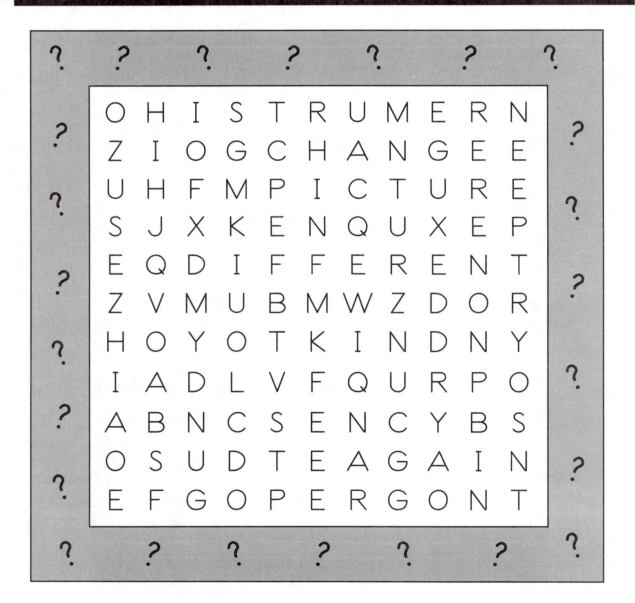

O H I S T R U M E R N
Z I O G C H A N G E E
U H F M P I C T U R E
S J X K E N Q U X E P
E Q D I F F E R E N T
Z V M U B M W Z D O R
H O Y O T K I N D N Y
I A D L V F Q U R P O
A B N C S E N C Y B S
O S U D T E A G A I N
E F G O P E R G O N T

Name _____

Choose the Correct Words

Directions: Choose the correct word to complete each sentence and write the word in the space.

different, home, us, move, try, kind, hand, picture, again, change

1. The giraffe will need to move to a _____ home.

   different   picture

2. This man is very _____ to the elephant.

   home   kind

3. The tiger will _____ to jump through it again.

   us   try

4. She will _____ that picture for another one.

   kind   change

5. This bear will try to _____ in here.

   move   change

6. The monkey will try to _____ it to us.

   hand   again

Name _____

Just-for-Fun Spelling

Directions: Cut apart the letters on this page. Use the letters to spell each of the words in the word box.

different, home, us, move, try, kind, hand, picture, again, change

a	a	c	d	e	e
f	f	g	h	i	k
m	n	o	p	r	s
t	u	v	y	d	p

158 © Teacher Created Materials, Inc.

Flashcards

Directions: Cut out the flashcards and use them to help you learn the words.

off, play, spell, air, away, animal, house, point, page, letter

off	animal
play	house
spell	point
air	page
away	letter

Write the Words

Directions: Write the words in the spaces.

| off, play, spell, air, away, animal, house, point, page, letter |

1. off _____

2. play _____

3. spell _____

4. air _____

5. away _____

6. animal _____

7. house _____

8. point _____

9. page _____

10. letter _____

Find the Words—Level A

Directions: There are 10 Instant Words hidden here. Can you find and circle them?

Here are the words to look for:

air, away, letter, page, point, animal, house, off, play, spell

```
S  I  H  O  U  S  E  O  C
L  E  T  T  E  R  M  D  X
C  V  W  L  N  N  T  P  O
P  O  F  F  N  L  B  U  D
A  W  A  Y  P  A  G  E  P
U  P  L  A  Y  C  P  V  I
S  P  E  L  L  A  I  R  T
A  N  I  M  A  L  H  W  E
X  P  O  I  N  T  M  U  J
```

Match Pictures with Sentences

Directions: Circle **a** or **b** to choose the sentence that best describes each picture.

off, play, away, animal, point, spell, air, house, page, letter

ball   doll   train   game   skateboard

1. 
   a. That animal must get off my skateboard!
   b. That animal must not write with my skateboard.

2.
   a. See her play with the ball.
   b. See her point at the new doll.

3. 
   a. They like to play their new game.
   b. They put the train away.

4.
   a. How do you spell your name?
   b. All these people are in my house.

5.
   a. Which page do you want to read?
   b. He just went through the air again.

6.
   a. She will live up in the air.
   b. She will write a letter to some people.

Name _____

Find the Words—Level B

Directions: There are 10 Instant Words hidden here. Can you find and circle them?

Here are the words to look for:

air, away, letter, page, point, animal, house, off, play, spell

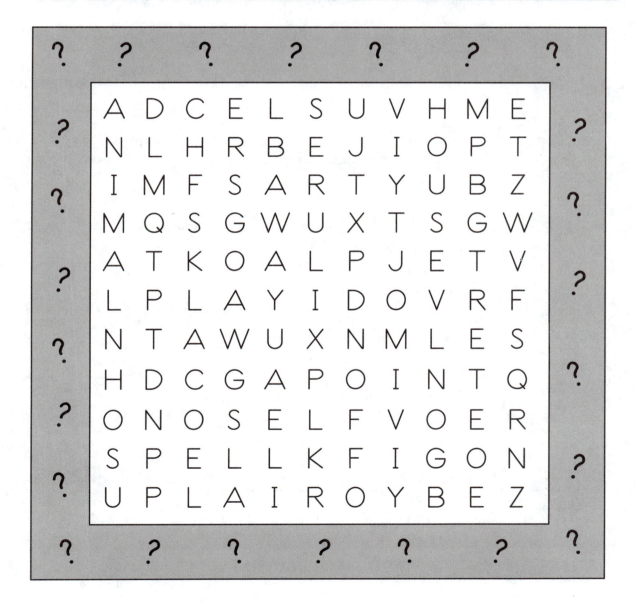

```
A D C E L S U V H M E
N L H R B E J I O P T
I M F S A R T Y U B Z
M Q S G W U X T S G W
A T K O A L P J E T V
L P L A Y I D O V R F
N T A W U X N M L E S
H D C G A P O I N T Q
O N O S E L F V O E R
S P E L L K F I G O N
U P L A I R O Y B E Z
```

Name _____

Choose the Correct Words

Directions: Choose the correct word to complete each sentence and write the word in the space.

off, play, spell, air, away, animal, house, point, page, letter

ball   doll   train   game   skateboard

1.   Can we _____ ball at your house?
   play point

2.   This _____ can look like a doll.
   page animal

3.   The _____ came to him on a train.
   spell letter

4.   His skateboard is up in the _____ .
   air away

5.   Turn it _____ after you play the game.
   off page

6.  We want this animal to go _____ .
   away house

Just-for-Fun Mystery Words

Be a detective! Can you use the code symbols to solve the mystery words?

Directions: Look at the code symbols under each line. Match each symbol to each letter and fill in the letters on each line. Check the words that you made to make sure they match the instant words in the box.

> off, play, spell, air, away, animal, house, point, page, letter

1. __ __ __ __ __ __
   ☆ □ ⊠ ⊠ □ ■

2. __ __ __
   ✳ × ■

3. __ __ __ __ __
   ◉ ● ▲ ♡ □

4. __ __ __ __ __
   ♡ ▫ □ ☆ ☆

5. __ __ __ __ __
   ▫ ● × → ⊠

6. __ __ __ __
   ▫ ☆ ✳ ★

7. __ __ __
   ● ↓ ↓

8. __ __ __ __
   ▫ ✳ ▼ □

9. __ __ __ __
   ✳ ◭ ✳ ★

10. __ __ __ __ __ __
    ✳ → × ♥ ✳ ☆

Code Symbols

a = ✳   b = △   c = ↑   d = ÷   e = □   f = ↓   g = ▼   h = ◉   i = ✕

j = ○   k = ▽   l = ☆   m = ♥   n = →   o = ●   p = ▫   q = ←   r = ■

s = ♡   t = ⊠   u = ▲   v = +   w = ◭   x = ❀   y = ★   z = ⊗

Unit 20

Flashcards

Directions: Cut out the flashcards and use them to help you learn the words.

mother, answer, found, study, still, learn, should, America, world, high

mother	learn
answer	should
found	America
study	world
still	high

Name _____  Unit 20

Write the Words

Directions: Write the words in the spaces.

mother, answer, found, study, still, learn, should, America, world, high

1. mother _____

2. answer _____

3. found _____

4. study _____

5. still _____

6. learn _____

7. should _____

8. America _____

9. world _____

10. high _____

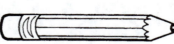

Name _____

Find the Words—Level A

Directions: There are 10 Instant Words hidden here. Can you find and circle them?

Here are the words to look for:

America, found, learn, should, study, answer, high, mother, still, world

D A M E R I C A R R
Y M O T H E R C O J
O X N C F O U N D T
S T U D Y S T I L L
L E A R N O H Y J D
H L R E F X Q M R O
H G I W O R L D L K
P D G C N P L X P B
H I G H A N S W E R
E T R S S H O U L D

168

Match Pictures with Sentences

Directions: Circle **a** or **b** to choose the sentence that best describes each picture.

mother, answer, found, still, should, study, learn, America, world, high

marker   scissors   paste   ruler   chalkboard

1.
    a. See him study that sentence.
    b. He is from a different world.

2.
    a. They will learn about America.
    b. There are no people in America.

3.
    a. Have you found the right answer?
    b. They should still be there.

4.
    a. His mother said he could have that marker.
    b. His mother said he could have the paste.

5.
    a. She will write the answer on the chalkboard.
    b. She will write the answer on the scissors.

6.
    a. I have my ruler.
    b. I have not found my ruler.

Unit 20

Find the Words—Level B

Directions: There are 10 Instant Words hidden here. Can you find and circle them?

Here are the words to look for:

America, found, learn, should, study, answer, high, mother, still, world

? ? ? ? ? ? ?

?

```
E L F O N S E N B O G
R A E R N E H I G H V
S M E A S O A O E F A
T K I H R D M B U C P
I N G O K N E S A L C
L F O U N D R V N B D
L C J R D L I U S J E
S T U D Y Q C T W E M
O I K E X J A N E B O
X O S M O T H E R T S
Z N A P T O W O R L D
```

? ? ? ? ? ? ?

Name _____

Choose the Correct Words

Directions: Choose the correct word to complete each sentence and write the word in the space.

mother, answer, found, study, still, learn, should, America, world, high

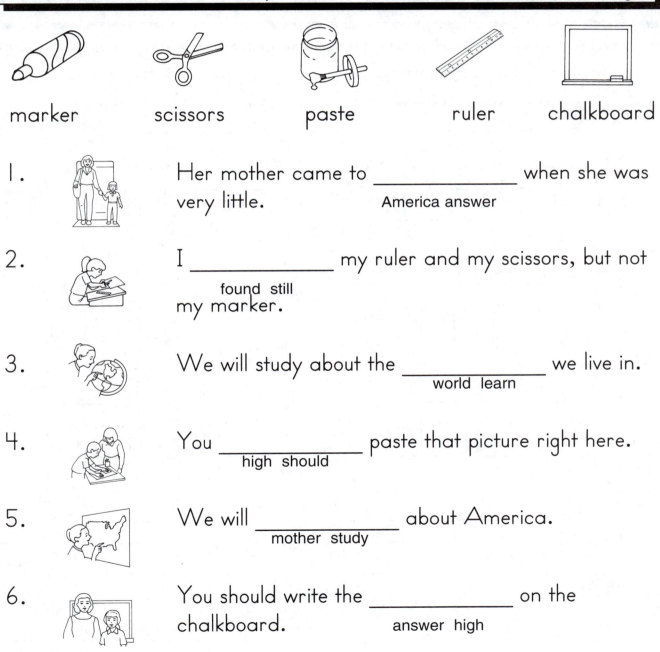

marker   scissors   paste   ruler   chalkboard

1. Her mother came to _____ when she was very little.
   America answer

2. I _____ my ruler and my scissors, but not
   found still
   my marker.

3. We will study about the _____ we live in.
   world learn

4. You _____ paste that picture right here.
   high should

5. We will _____ about America.
   mother study

6. You should write the _____ on the chalkboard.
   answer high

Name _____

Just-for-Fun Letter Squares

Directions: Write the missing letters in the squares to spell the words from the word box. Then copy the completed words on the lines below the squares.

mother, answer, found, study, still, learn, should, America, world, high

1. ☐f☐ ☐ ☐ ☐ ☐

_____

2. ☐ ☐ ☐ ☐l ☐l ☐

_____

3. ☐ ☐ ☐t ☐h ☐ ☐

_____

4. ☐ ☐ ☐ ☐ ☐y ☐

_____

5. ☐s ☐h ☐ ☐ ☐ ☐

_____

6. ☐h ☐ ☐ ☐

_____

7. ☐a ☐n ☐ ☐ ☐ ☐

_____

8. ☐l ☐ ☐ ☐ ☐

_____

9. ☐ ☐o ☐r ☐ ☐

_____

10. ☐ ☐ ☐ ☐ ☐c ☐a

_____

Unit 21

Flashcards

Directions: Cut out the flashcards and use them to help you learn the words.

every, near, add, food, between, own, below, country, plant, last

every	own
near	below
add	country
food	plant
between	last

Name _____

Write the Words

Directions: Write the words in the spaces.

every, near, add, food, between, own, below, country, plant, last

1. every _____

_____

2. near _____

_____

3. add _____

_____

4. food _____

_____

5. between _____

_____

6. own _____

_____

7. below _____

_____

8. country _____

_____

9. plant _____

_____

10. last _____

_____

Find the Words–Level A

Directions: There are 10 Instant Words hidden here. Can you find and circle them?

Here are the words to look for:

add, between, every, last, own, below, country, food, near, plant

```
L A S T U O E L M I
B E T W E E N D S P
Q B U L D P L A N T
T V R O W N A R M U
N E A R B E L O W A
A U Q A D D J I R B
F O O D E V E R Y Q
U T E L V G B Q O Q
G Y T S I I P K I A
O C O U N T R Y O L
```

Name _____

Write the Words in Sentences

Directions: Choose a word from the word box to complete each sentence and write the word in the space. More than one word from the word box may fit some sentences.

every, between, below, plant, last, near, add, food, own, country

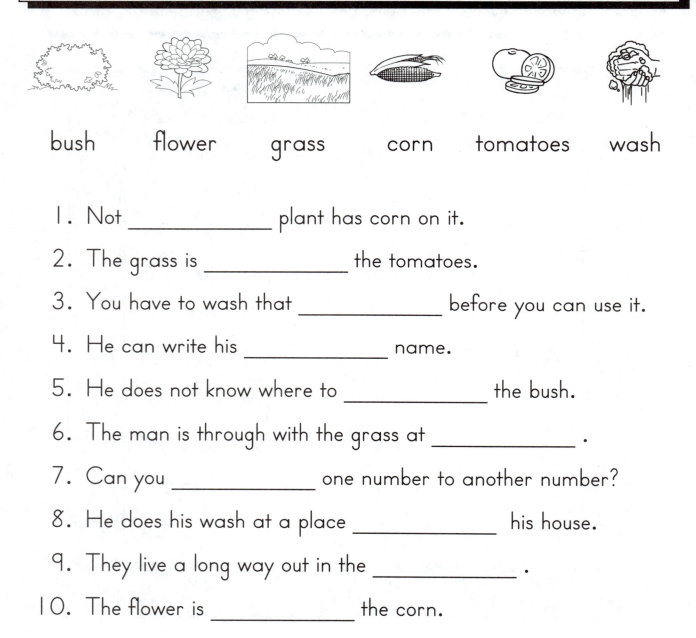

bush   flower   grass   corn   tomatoes   wash

1. Not _____ plant has corn on it.

2. The grass is _____ the tomatoes.

3. You have to wash that _____ before you can use it.

4. He can write his _____ name.

5. He does not know where to _____ the bush.

6. The man is through with the grass at _____ .

7. Can you _____ one number to another number?

8. He does his wash at a place _____ his house.

9. They live a long way out in the _____ .

10. The flower is _____ the corn.

Name _____

Find the Words—Level B

Directions: There are 10 Instant Words hidden here. Can you find and circle them?

Here are the words to look for:

below, country, food, near, plant, add, between, every, last, own

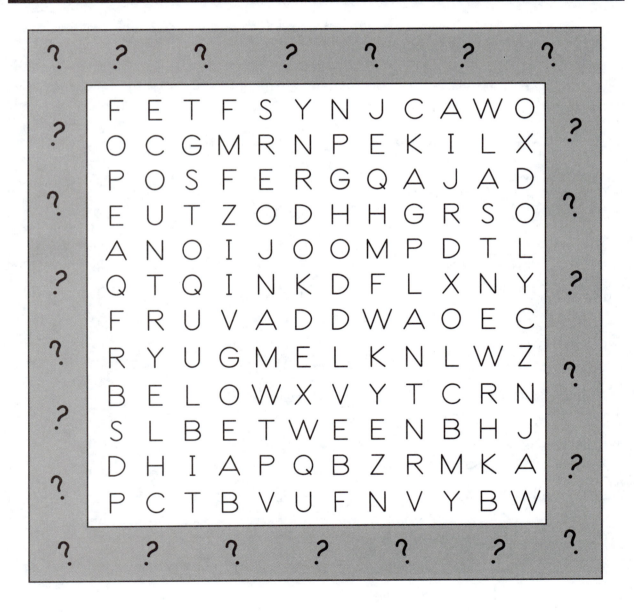

```
F E T F S Y N J C A W O
O C G M R N P E K I L X
P O S F E R G Q A J A D
E U T Z O D H H G R S O
A N O I J O O M P D T L
Q T Q I N K D F L X N Y
F R U V A D D W A O E C
R Y U G M E L K N L W Z
B E L O W X V Y T C R N
S L B E T W E E N B H J
D H I A P Q B Z R M K A
P C T B V U F N V Y B W
```

Name _____

Choose the Correct Words

Directions: Choose the correct word to complete each sentence and write the word in the space.

every, near, add, food, between, own, below, country, plant, last

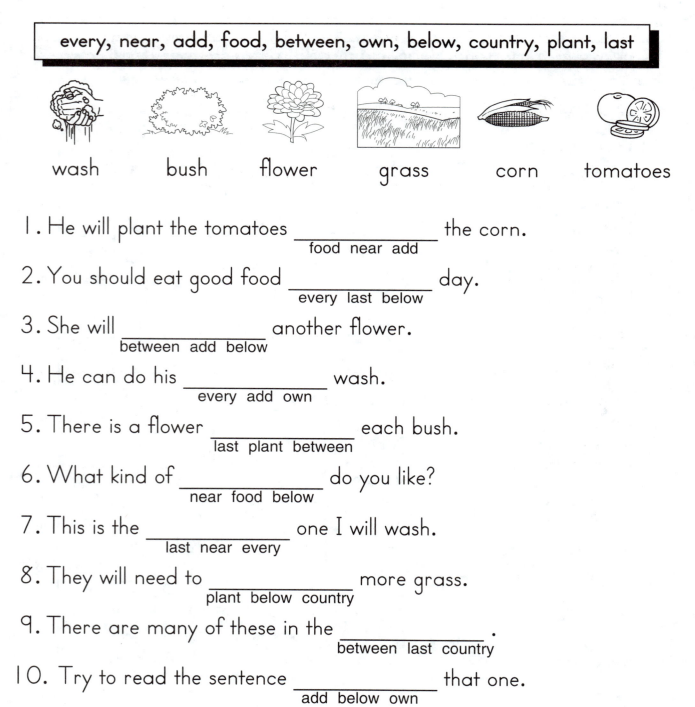

wash   bush   flower   grass   corn   tomatoes

1. He will plant the tomatoes _____ the corn.
   food near add

2. You should eat good food _____ day.
   every last below

3. She will _____ another flower.
   between add below

4. He can do his _____ wash.
   every add own

5. There is a flower _____ each bush.
   last plant between

6. What kind of _____ do you like?
   near food below

7. This is the _____ one I will wash.
   last near every

8. They will need to _____ more grass.
   plant below country

9. There are many of these in the _____.
   between last country

10. Try to read the sentence _____ that one.
    add below own

Unit 21

Just-for-Fun Word Scramble

Directions: Unscramble the mixed-up words below. Write the correct word from the word box on each line.

| every, near, add, food, between, own, below, country, plant, last |

1. tnlap _____

2. nwo _____

3. dda _____

4. odfo _____

5. wobel _____

6. veyre _____

7. wenebet _____

8. atsl _____

9. tuncyro _____

10. erna _____

Flashcards

Directions: Cut out the flashcards and use them to help you learn the words.

school, father, keep, tree, never, start, city, earth, eye, light

school	start
father	city
keep	earth
tree	eye
never	light

Name _____

Write the Words

Directions: Write the words in the spaces.

| school, father, keep, tree, never, start, city, earth, eye, light |

1. school _____

_____

2. father _____

_____

3. keep _____

_____

4. tree _____

_____

5. never _____

_____

6. start _____

_____

7. city _____

_____

8. earth _____

_____

9. eye _____

_____

10. light _____

_____

Find the Words–Level A

Directions: There are 10 Instant Words hidden here. Can you find and circle them?

Here are the words to look for:

city, eye, keep, never, start, earth, father, light, school, tree

Name _____

Unit 22

Write the Words in Sentences

Directions: Choose a word from the word box to complete each sentence and write the word in the space.

| school, never, city, earth, light, father, keep, tree, start, eye |

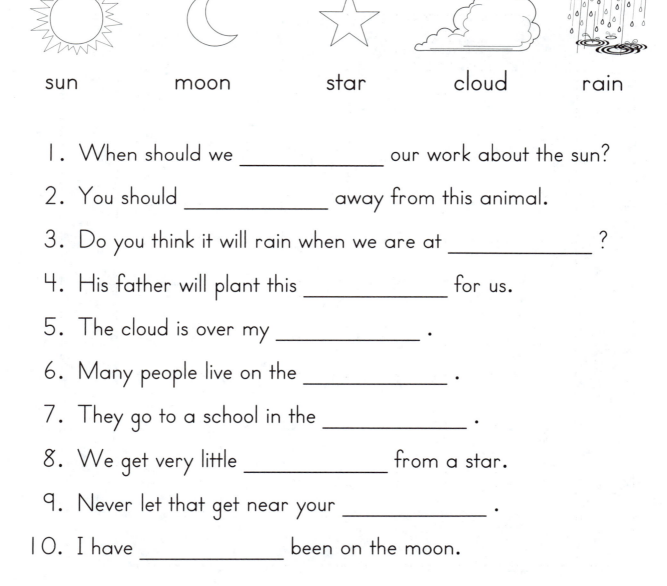

sun   moon   star   cloud   rain

1. When should we _____ our work about the sun?

2. You should _____ away from this animal.

3. Do you think it will rain when we are at _____ ?

4. His father will plant this _____ for us.

5. The cloud is over my _____ .

6. Many people live on the _____ .

7. They go to a school in the _____ .

8. We get very little _____ from a star.

9. Never let that get near your _____ .

10. I have _____ been on the moon.

Name _____  Unit 22

Find the Words—Level B

Directions: There are 10 Instant Words hidden here. Can you find and circle them?

Here are the words to look for:

earth, father, light, school, tree, city, eye, keep, never, start

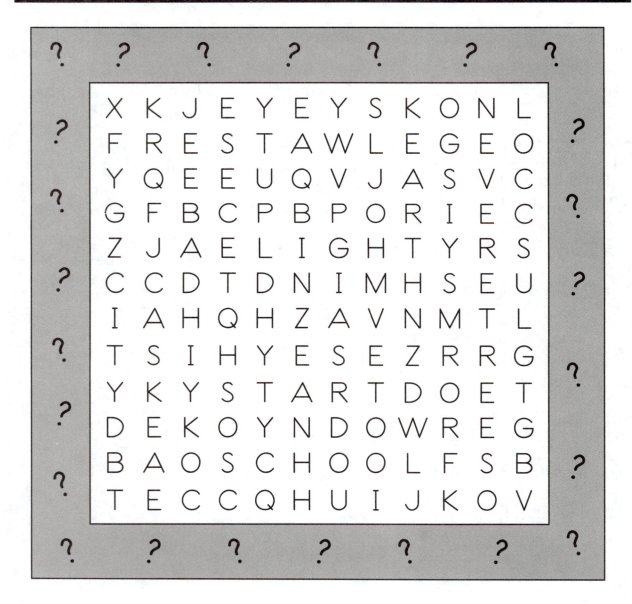

Name _____

Choose the Correct Words

Directions: Choose the correct word to complete each sentence and write the word in the space.

school, father, keep, tree, never, start, city, earth, eye, light

sun   moon   star   cloud   rain

1. It may _____ to rain.
   light start keep

2. Some people went from the _____ to the moon.
   earth tree eye

3. This plant will need _____ from the sun.
   eye light earth

4. Our _____ will take us to school.
   city light father

5. This _____ is very large.
   never start tree

6. Do not get that in your _____ .
   eye keep start

7. There is a big cloud over their _____ .
   school never start

8. People have _____ been to a star.
   earth never keep

9. They will move from the _____ to the country.
   school never city

10. You must _____ your hand away from this.
    father keep city

Name _____

Just-for-Fun Missing Letters

Directions: The words on the shirts are each missing a letter. Fill in the missing letters to spell the words from the word box. Then copy the completed words on the lines below the shirts.

| school, father, keep, tree, never, start, city, earth, eye, light |

1. sc _ ool

_____

2. nev _ r

_____

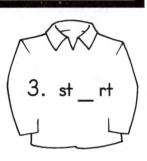

3. st _ rt

_____

4. e _ e

_____

5. ke _ p

_____

6. fa _ her

_____

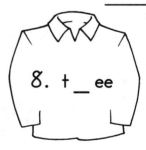

8. t _ ee

_____

7. e _ rth

_____

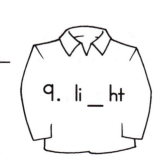

9. li _ ht

_____

10. cit _

_____

Flashcards

Directions: Cut out the flashcards and use them to help you learn the words.

thought, head, under, story, saw, left, don't, few, while, along

thought	left
head	don't
under	few
story	while
saw	along

Write the Words

Directions: Write the words in the spaces.

| thought, head, under, story, saw, left, don't, few, while, along |

1. thought _____

_____

2. head _____

_____

3. under _____

_____

4. story _____

_____

5. saw _____

_____

6. left _____

_____

7. don't _____

_____

8. few _____

_____

9. while _____

_____

10. along _____

_____

Name _____

Find the Words—Level A

Directions: There are 10 Instant Words hidden here. Can you find and circle them?

Here are the words to look for:

along, few, left, story, under, don't, head, saw, thought, while

```
G M Y S A W G O P F
D E V O B A W P K M
Q Q A J R Y D O N T
O P G D W V J F E W
I G B J C C I E K S
G P N U N D E R Q J
W R M S T O R Y B W
B A W H I L E M I W
L E F T H O U G H T
A L O N G H E A D E
```

Write the Words in Sentences

Directions: Choose a word from the word box to complete each sentence and write the word in the space.

story, saw, left, few, along, thought, head, under, don't, while

cat   dog   rabbit   bird   fish   sleep

1. His father read him a _____ about a rabbit.

2. There are only a few fish _____ .

3. She _____ their dog go after her cat.

4. Follow _____ and go where we go.

5. Only a _____ people were there.

6. She will want to sleep for a _____ .

7. Is that a bird on his _____ ?

8. _____ sleep too long.

9. Don't put your head _____ there!

10. He _____ of a good story to read.

Find the Words—Level B

Directions: There are 10 Instant Words hidden here. Can you find and circle them?

Here are the words to look for:

along, few, left, story, under, don't, head, saw, thought, while

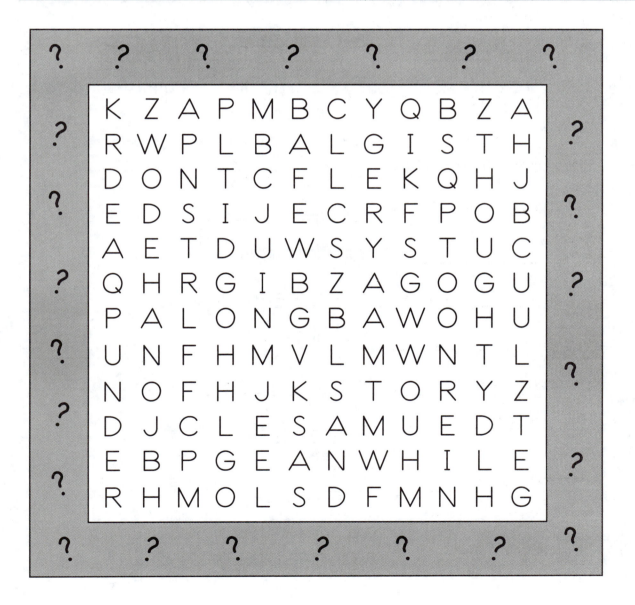

```
K Z A P M B C Y Q B Z A
R W P L B A L G I S T H
D O N T C F L E K Q H J
E D S I J E C R F P O B
A E T D U W S Y S T U C
Q H R G I B Z A G O G U
P A L O N G B A W O H U
U N F H M V L M W N T L
N O F H J K S T O R Y Z
D J C L E S A M U E D T
E B P G E A N W H I L E
R H M O L S D F M N H G
```

Name _____  Unit 23

Choose the Correct Words

Directions: Choose the correct word to complete each sentence and write the word in the space.

thought, head, under, story, saw, left, don't, few, while, along

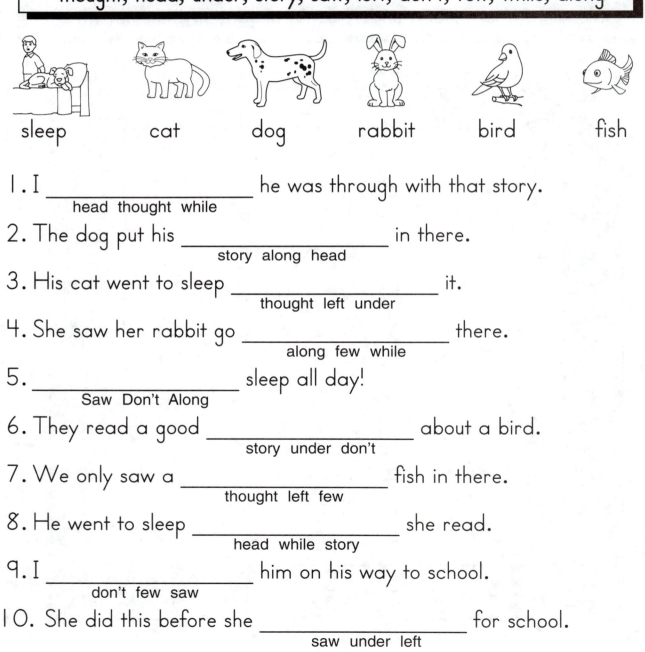

sleep   cat   dog   rabbit   bird   fish

1. I _____ he was through with that story.
   head thought while

2. The dog put his _____ in there.
   story along head

3. His cat went to sleep _____ it.
   thought left under

4. She saw her rabbit go _____ there.
   along few while

5. _____ sleep all day!
   Saw Don't Along

6. They read a good _____ about a bird.
   story under don't

7. We only saw a _____ fish in there.
   thought left few

8. He went to sleep _____ she read.
   head while story

9. I _____ him on his way to school.
   don't few saw

10. She did this before she _____ for school.
    saw under left

Name _____

Just-for-Fun Spelling

Directions: Cut apart the letters and the apostrophe on this page. Use the letters to spell each of the words in the word box.

thought, head, under, story, saw, left, don't, few, while, along

a	d	e	f	g
h	h	i	l	n
o	r	s	t	t
’	u	w	y	o

Flashcards

Directions: Cut out the flashcards and use them to help you learn the words.

might, close, something, seem, next, hard, open, example, begin, life

might	hard
close	open
something	example
seem	begin
next	life

Write the Words

Directions: Write the words in the spaces.

might, close, something, seem, next, hard, open, example, begin, life

1. might _____

2. close _____

3. something _____

4. seem _____

5. next _____

6. hard _____

7. open _____

8. example _____

9. begin _____

10. life _____

Name _____

Find the Words—Level A

Directions: There are 10 Instant Words hidden here. Can you find and circle them?

Here are the words to look for:

| begin, example, life, next, seem, close, hard, might, open, something |

```
L M I G H T Y A S E E M
S L I F E C L O S E R P
B E G I N M V E D F E K
H A R D X W H B L F P B
M P J S O M E T H I N G
B O P E N E X T N X J B
F C D Z D S C N U F L K
O A E X A M P L E O H M
S A S Q Z C B D Z F L J
F Z H S K N B Y Z L B L
E D M A D Y W I H N H B
X R E V J Q E X A I K P
```

Write the Words in Sentences

Directions: Choose a word from the word box to complete each sentence and write the word in the space. More than one word from the word box may fit some sentences.

might, close, something, hard, open, seem, next, example, begin, life

farmer   police officer   cook   doctor   nurse

1. The cook will make _____ good for us.

2. It does not _____ as if the nurse is that old.

3. It is his turn _____ .

4. You may _____ work now.

5. A farmer has to work very _____ .

6. This sentence is a good _____ .

7. She will write a story about her _____ .

8. The police officer cannot _____ it.

9. The doctor said for him to keep his eye _____ .

10. He _____ get this one right.

Name _____

Unit 24

Find the Words—Level B

Directions: There are 10 Instant Words hidden here. Can you find and circle them?

Here are the words to look for:

close, hard, might, open, something, begin, example, life, next, seem

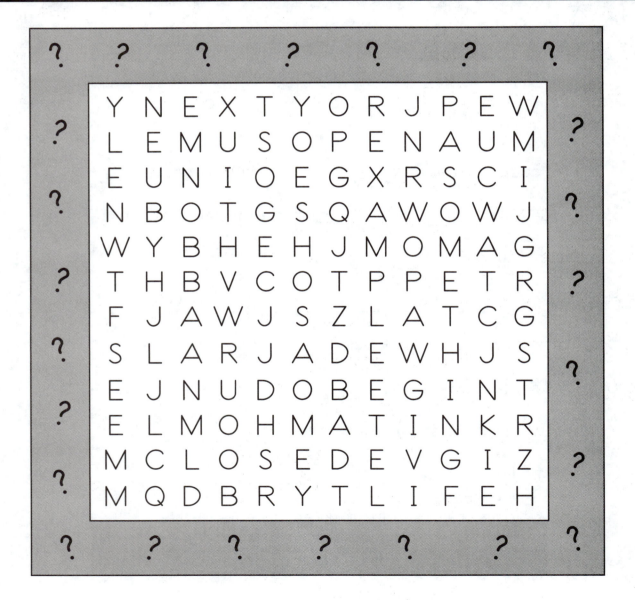

```
Y N E X T Y O R J P E W
L E M U S O P E N A U M
E U N I O E G X R S C I
N B O T G S Q A W O W J
W Y B H E H J M O M A G
T H B V C O T P P E T R
F J A W J S Z L A T C G
S L A R J A D E W H J S
E J N U D O B E G I N T
E L M O H M A T I N K R
M C L O S E D E V G I Z
M Q D B R Y T L I F E H
```

Name _____

Choose the Correct Words

Directions: Choose the correct word to complete each sentence and write the word in the space.

might, close, something, seem, next, hard, open, example, begin, life

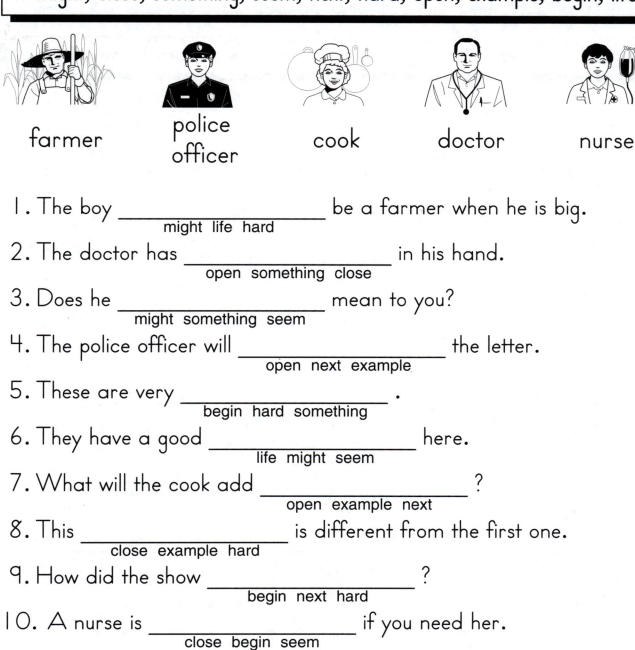

farmer   police officer   cook   doctor   nurse

1. The boy _____ be a farmer when he is big.
   might life hard

2. The doctor has _____ in his hand.
   open something close

3. Does he _____ mean to you?
   might something seem

4. The police officer will _____ the letter.
   open next example

5. These are very _____ .
   begin hard something

6. They have a good _____ here.
   life might seem

7. What will the cook add _____ ?
   open example next

8. This _____ is different from the first one.
   close example hard

9. How did the show _____ ?
   begin next hard

10. A nurse is _____ if you need her.
    close begin seem

Just-for-Fun Mystery Words

Be a detective! Can you use the code symbols to solve the mystery words?

Directions: Look at the code symbols under each line. Match each symbol to each letter and fill in the letters on each line. Check the words that you made to make sure they match the instant words in the box.

might, close, something, seem, next, hard, open, example, begin, life

1. s o m e t h i n g
♡ ● ♥ □ ⊠ ⊙ ✕ → ▼

6. b e g i n
△ □ ▼ ✕ →

2. l i f e
☆ ✕ ↓ □

7. m i g h t
♥ ✕ ▼ ⊙ ⊠

3. s e e m
♡ □ □ ♥

8. c l o s e
↑ ☆ ● ♡ □

4. o p e n
● ⊡ □ →

9. h a r d
⊙ ✳ ■ ÷

5. e x a m p l e
□ ❀ ✳ ♥ ⊡ ☆ □

10. n e x t
→ □ ❀ ⊠

Code Symbols

a = ✳ b = △ c = ↑ d = ÷ e = □ f = ↓ g = ▼ h = ⊙ i = ✕

j = ○ k = ▽ l = ☆ m = ♥ n = → o = ● p = ⊡ q = ← r = ■

s = ♡ t = ⊠ u = ▲ v = + w = ◮ x = ❀ y = ★ z = ⊗

200

Name _____

Flashcards

Directions: Cut out the flashcards and use them to help you learn the words.

always, those, both, paper, together, got, group, often, run, important

always	got
those	group
both	often
paper	run
together	important

Name _____  Unit 25

Write the Words

Directions: Write the words in the spaces.

always, those, both, paper, together, got, group, often, run, important

1. always _____

2. those _____

3. both _____

4. paper _____

5. together _____

6. got _____

7. group _____

8. often _____

9. run _____

10. important _____

Find the Words—Level A

Directions: There are 10 Instant Words hidden here. Can you find and circle them?

Here are the words to look for:

always, got, important, paper, those, both, group, often, run, together

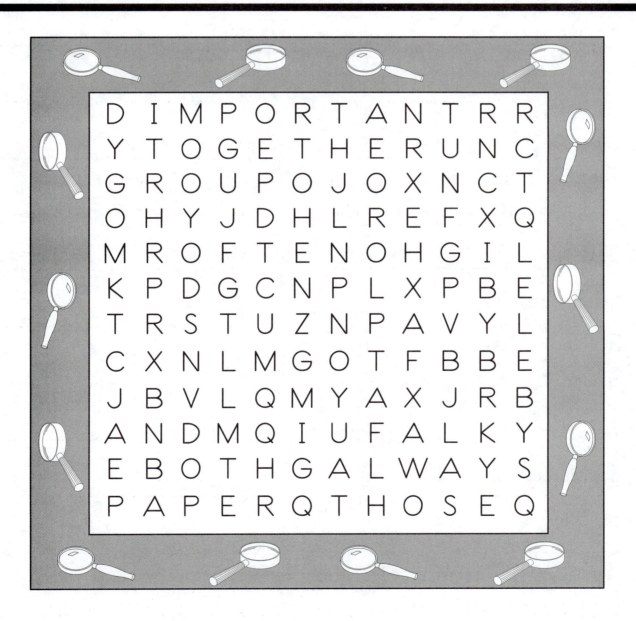

```
D I M P O R T A N T R R
Y T O G E T H E R U N C
G R O U P O J O X N C T
O H Y J D H L R E F X Q
M R O F T E N O H G I L
K P D G C N P L X P B E
T R S T U Z N P A V Y L
C X N L M G O T F B B E
J B V L Q M Y A X J R B
A N D M Q I U F A L K Y
E B O T H G A L W A Y S
P A P E R Q T H O S E Q
```

Name _____

Write the Words in Sentences

Directions: Choose a word from the word box to complete each sentence and write the word in the space.

both, group, often, run, important, always, those, paper, together, got

horse   cow   pig   chicken   duck

1. This horse can _____ very well.

2 The cow _____ away.

3. It is _____ to study hard.

4. They play here _____ .

5. That chicken got away from the _____ .

6. The pig and the duck are _____ his.

7. I don't _____ know the right answer.

8. He cannot put that thing _____ .

9. She has no more _____ .

10. Can I have some of _____ ?

Name _____  Unit 25

Find the Words–Level B

Directions: There are 10 Instant Words hidden here. Can you find and circle them?

Here are the words to look for:

| always, got, important, paper, those, both, group, often, run, together |

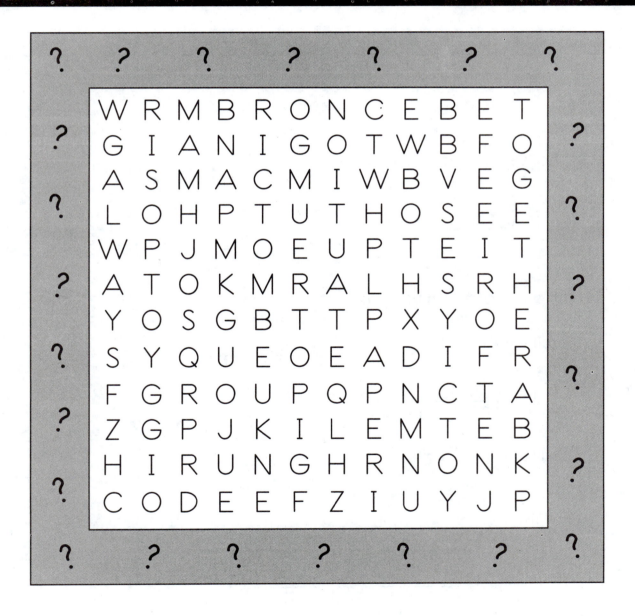

Name _____

Choose the Correct Words

Directions: Choose the correct word to complete each sentence and write the word in the space.

always, those, both, paper, together, got, group, often, run, important

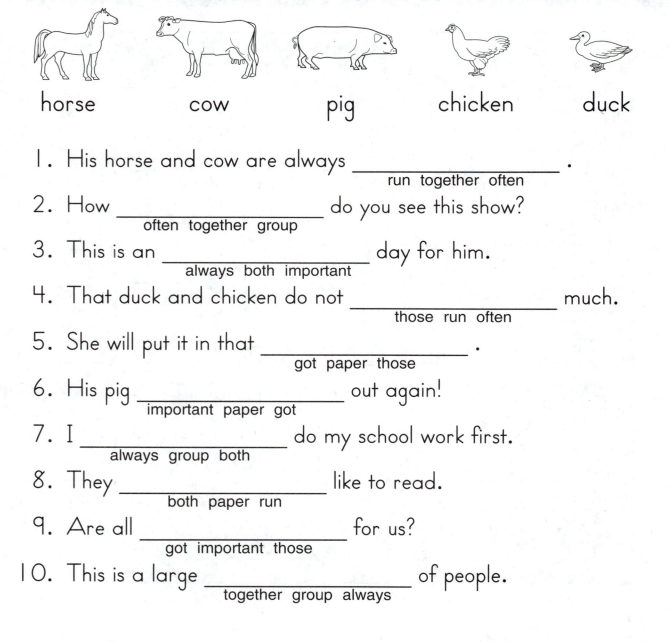

horse   cow   pig   chicken   duck

1. His horse and cow are always _____ .
   run together often

2. How _____ do you see this show?
   often together group

3. This is an _____ day for him.
   always both important

4. That duck and chicken do not _____ much.
   those run often

5. She will put it in that _____ .
   got paper those

6. His pig _____ out again!
   important paper got

7. I _____ do my school work first.
   always group both

8. They _____ like to read.
   both paper run

9. Are all _____ for us?
   got important those

10. This is a large _____ of people.
    together group always

Name _____  Unit 25

Just-for-Fun Letter Squares

Directions: Write the missing letters in the squares to spell the words from the word box. Then copy the completed words on the lines below the squares.

always, those, both, paper, together, got, group, often, run, important

1. ☐ ☐ t h
   _____

2. t h ☐ ☐ ☐
   _____

3. ☐ o ☐
   _____

4. a l ☐ ☐ ☐ ☐
   _____

5. g r ☐ ☐ ☐
   _____

6. ☐ u ☐
   _____

7. ☐ ☐ ☐ e r
   _____

8. o f ☐ ☐ ☐
   _____

9. t o ☐ ☐ ☐ ☐ ☐
   _____

10. ☐ ☐ ☐ ☐ ☐ ☐ ☐ t
    _____

Flashcards

Directions: Cut out the flashcards and use them to help you learn the words.

until, children, side, feet, car, mile, night, walk, white, sea

until	mile
children	night
side	walk
feet	white
car	sea

Write the Words

Directions: Write the words in the spaces.

until, children, side, feet, car, mile, night, walk, white, sea

1. until _____

_____

2. children _____

_____

3. side _____

_____

4. feet _____

_____

5. car _____

_____

6. mile _____

_____

7. night _____

_____

8. walk _____

_____

9. white _____

_____

10. sea _____

_____

Unit 26

Find the Words—Level A

Directions: There are 10 Instant Words hidden here. Can you find and circle them?

Here are the words to look for:

car, feet, night, side, walk, children, mile, sea, until, white

C A R Q I W W H I T E
D D M W P F E O J V D
P Q O J R O K Z L Y D
N I G H T D F E E T M
W A L K H M I L E R H
N N G R S S Y G P O D
C H I L D R E N S E A
X W K D U N T I L M L
V H P J K D T H E G L
K F B P O S I D E T W
N A U A O L Y Q H W X

Name _____

Write the Words in Sentences

Directions: Choose a word from the word box to complete each sentence and write the word in the space.

until, car, mile, walk, sea, children, side, feet, night, white

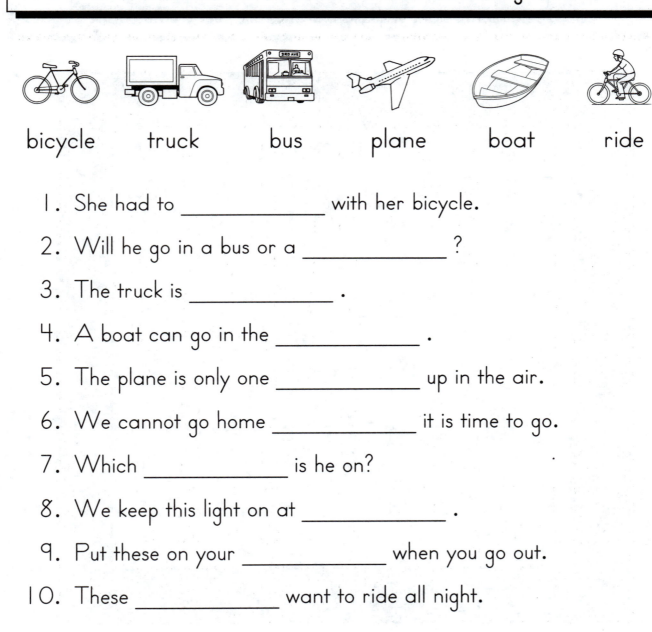

bicycle   truck   bus   plane   boat   ride

1. She had to _____ with her bicycle.

2. Will he go in a bus or a _____ ?

3. The truck is _____ .

4. A boat can go in the _____ .

5. The plane is only one _____ up in the air.

6. We cannot go home _____ it is time to go.

7. Which _____ is he on?

8. We keep this light on at _____ .

9. Put these on your _____ when you go out.

10. These _____ want to ride all night.

Find the Words—Level B

Directions: There are 10 Instant Words hidden here. Can you find and circle them?

Here are the words to look for:

car, feet, night, side, walk, children, mile, sea, until, white

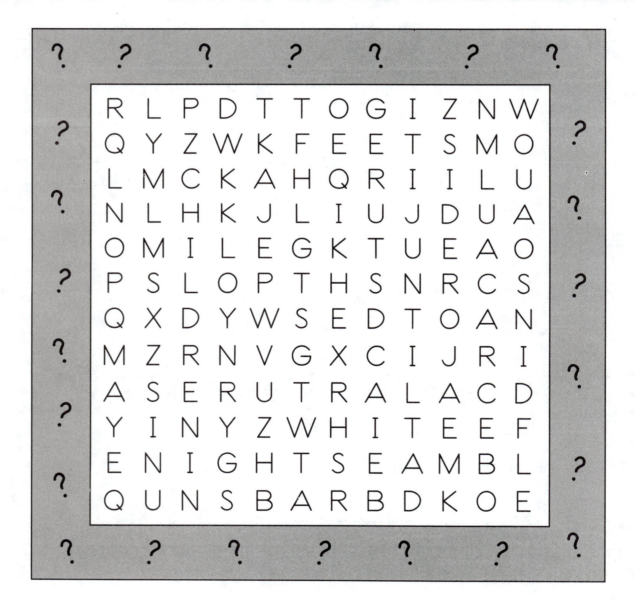

Choose the Correct Words

Directions: Choose the correct word to complete each sentence and write the word in the space.

until, children, side, feet, car, mile, night, walk, white, sea

ride   bicycle   truck   bus   plane   boat

1. When will he learn to _____ ?
   feet sea walk

2. These children got to play by the _____ .
   feet sea night

3. This _____ boat is very large.
   white side walk

4. Will she ride in a bus, plane, or _____ ?
   mile until car

5. These _____ can each ride a bicycle.
   children feet side

6. Her hand is on her left _____ .
   children side white

7. How many _____ long is that truck?
   car walk feet

8. They will ride _____ they get there.
   mile night until

9. We do not see this light at _____ .
   night until children

10. She has run one _____ .
    white sea mile

Just-for-Fun Word Scramble

Directions: Unscramble the mixed-up words below. Write the correct word from the word box on each line.

until, children, side, feet, car, mile, night, walk, white, sea

1. tefe _____

2. liem _____

3. hiwet _____

4. lutin _____

5. ase _____

6. drehinlc _____

7. ghint _____

8. acr _____

9. desi _____

10. alkw _____

Name _____

Flashcards

Directions: Cut out the flashcards and use them to help you learn the words.

began, grow, took, river, four, carry, state, once, book, hear

began	carry
grow	state
took	once
river	book
four	hear

Write the Words

Directions: Write the words in the spaces.

began, grow, took, river, four, carry, state, once, book, hear

1. began _____

2. grow _____

3. took _____

4. river _____

5. four _____

6. carry _____

7. state _____

8. once _____

9. book _____

10. hear _____

Unit 27

Find the Words—Level A

Directions: There are 10 Instant Words hidden here. Can you find and circle them?

Here are the words to look for:

> began, carry, grow, once, state, book, four, hear, river, took

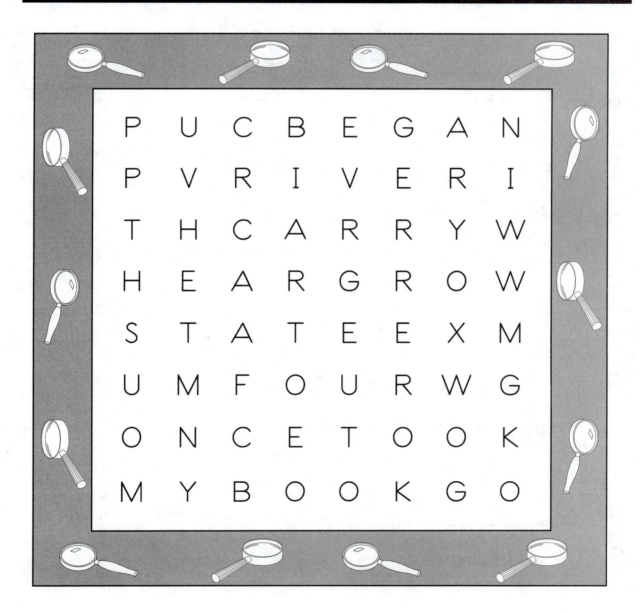

```
P  U  C  B  E  G  A  N
P  V  R  I  V  E  R  I
T  H  C  A  R  R  Y  W
H  E  A  R  G  R  O  W
S  T  A  T  E  E  X  M
U  M  F  O  U  R  W  G
O  N  C  E  T  O  O  K
M  Y  B  O  O  K  G  O
```

Write the Words in Sentences

Directions: Choose a word from the word box to complete each sentence and write the word in the space.

took, four, carry, book, hear, began, grow, river, state, once

table   chair   sofa   chest   desk   sit

1. Where will he _____ that chair?

2. The boy will read the _____ at his desk.

3. It _____ four men to carry the chest.

4. Do you _____ that sound?

5. There are _____ children on the sofa.

6. The children like to sit by the _____ .

7. The plant on the table began to _____ .

8. They will move to another _____ .

9. _____ you get there you will know where you are.

10. This is how the story _____ .

Name _____

Unit 27

Find the Words–Level B

Directions: There are 10 Instant Words hidden here. Can you find and circle them?

Here are the words to look for:

began, carry, grow, once, state, book, four, hear, river, took

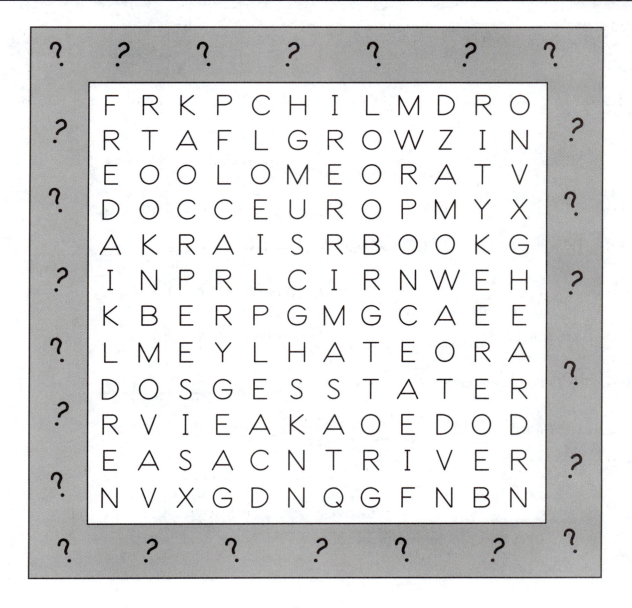

```
F R K P C H I L M D R O
R T A F L G R O W Z I N
E O O L O M E O R A T V
D O C C E U R O P M Y X
A K R A I S R B O O K G
I N P R L C I R N W E H
K B E R P G M G C A E E
L M E Y L H A T E O R A
D O S G E S S T A T E R
R V I E A K A O E D O D
E A S A C N T R I V E R
N V X G D N Q G F N B N
```

Name _____  Unit 27

Choose the Correct Words

Directions: Choose the correct word to complete each sentence and write the word in the space.

began, grow, took, river, four, carry, state, once, book, hear

sit   table   chair   sofa   chest   desk

1. We are from this _____ .
   river state book

2. Where will the men _____ that desk?
   carry grow once

3. They like to sit on the sofa and read a _____ .
   four book near

4. All _____ of them can sit at the table.
   began carry four

5. This show _____ before I got here.
   once hear began

6. He can sit in an old chair by the _____ .
   river four state

7. The plant began to _____ by the tree.
   took book grow

8. They _____ the chest in last.
   took state grow

9. We cannot _____ her read.
   carry hear took

10. Come here at _____ !
    began river once

Name _____

Unit 27

Just-for-Fun Missing Letters

Directions: The words on the apples are each missing a letter. Fill in the missing letters to spell the words from the word box. Then copy the completed words on the lines below the apples.

| began, grow, took, river, four, carry, state, once, book, hear |

1. car __ y

2. stat __

3. to __ k

_____

_____

_____

4. b __ ok

5. riv __ r

6. be __ an

_____

_____

_____

8. he __ r

10. fo __ r

7. __ nce

9. gro __

_____

_____

_____

Flashcards

Directions: Cut out the flashcards and use them to help you learn the words.

stop, without, second, late, miss, idea, enough, eat, face, watch

stop	idea
without	enough
second	eat
late	face
miss	watch

Write the Words

Directions: Write the words in the spaces.

stop, without, second, late, miss, idea, enough, eat, face, watch

1. stop _____

2. without _____

3. second _____

4. late _____

5. miss _____

6. idea _____

7. enough _____

8. eat _____

9. face _____

10. watch _____

Find the Words—Level A

Directions: There are 10 Instant Words hidden here. Can you find and circle them?

Here are the words to look for:

eat, face, late, second, watch, enough, idea, miss, stop, without

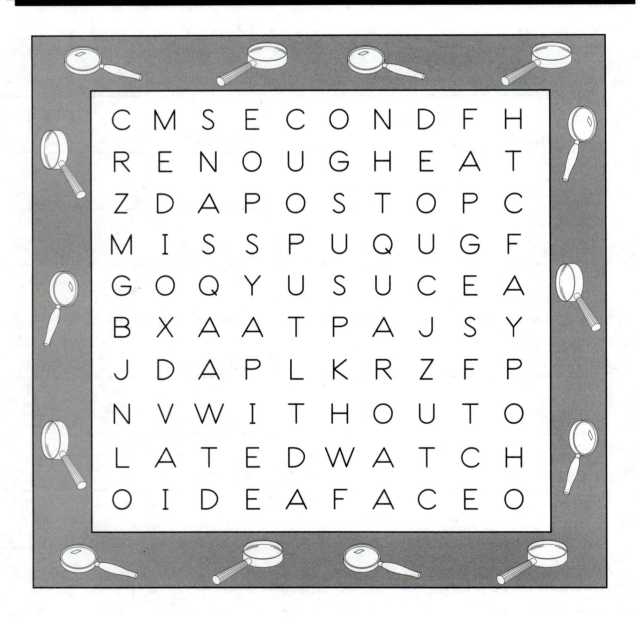

C M S E C O N D F H
R E N O U G H E A T
Z D A P O S T O P C
M I S S P U Q U G F
G O Q Y U S U C E A
B X A A T P A J S Y
J D A P L K R Z F P
N V W I T H O U T O
L A T E D W A T C H
O I D E A F A C E O

Write the Words in Sentences

Directions: Choose a word from the word box to complete each sentence and write the word in the space. More than one word from the word box may fit some sentences.

late, miss, enough, eat, watch, stop, without, second, idea, face

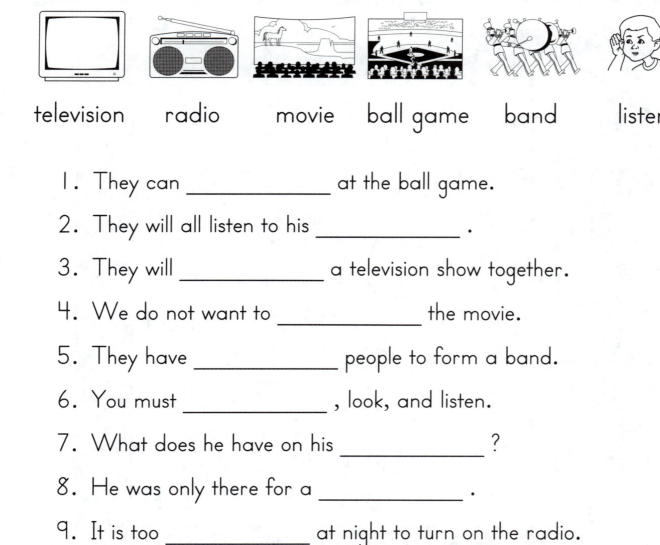

television   radio   movie   ball game   band   listen

1. They can _____ at the ball game.

2. They will all listen to his _____ .

3. They will _____ a television show together.

4. We do not want to _____ the movie.

5. They have _____ people to form a band.

6. You must _____ , look, and listen.

7. What does he have on his _____ ?

8. He was only there for a _____ .

9. It is too _____ at night to turn on the radio.

10. Don't go out _____ something on your feet.

Find the Words—Level B

Directions: There are 10 Instant Words hidden here. Can you find and circle them?

Here are the words to look for:

eat, face, late, second, watch, enough, idea, miss, stop, without

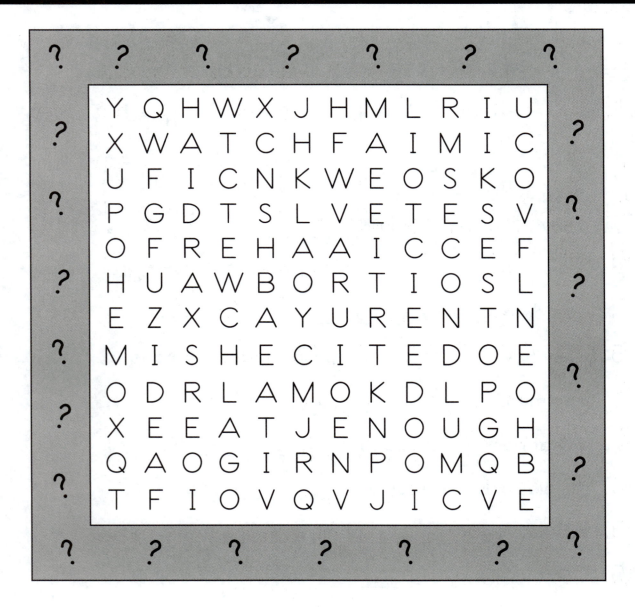

Name _____

Choose the Correct Words

Directions: Choose the correct word to complete each sentence and write the word in the space.

stop, without, second, late, miss, idea, enough, eat, face, watch

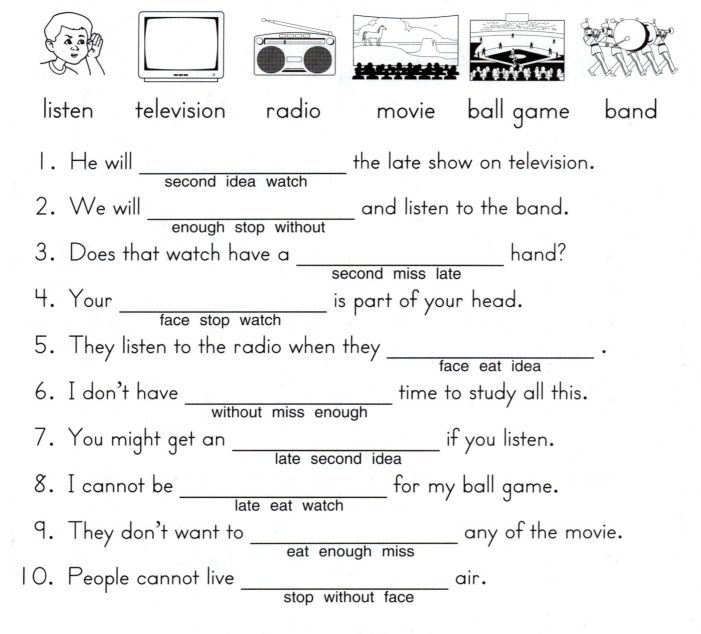

listen   television   radio   movie   ball game   band

1. He will _____ the late show on television.
   second idea watch

2. We will _____ and listen to the band.
   enough stop without

3. Does that watch have a _____ hand?
   second miss late

4. Your _____ is part of your head.
   face stop watch

5. They listen to the radio when they _____ .
   face eat idea

6. I don't have _____ time to study all this.
   without miss enough

7. You might get an _____ if you listen.
   late second idea

8. I cannot be _____ for my ball game.
   late eat watch

9. They don't want to _____ any of the movie.
   eat enough miss

10. People cannot live _____ air.
    stop without face

Just-for-Fun Spelling

Directions: Cut apart the letters on this page. Use the letters to spell each of the words in the word box.

stop, without, second, late, miss, idea, enough, eat, face, watch

a	c	d	e	f
g	h	i	l	m
n	o	p	s	s
t	t	u	w	i

228

Flashcards

Directions: Cut out the flashcards and use them to help you learn the words.

far, Indian, real, almost, let, above, girl, sometimes, mountain, cut

far	above
Indian	girl
real	sometimes
almost	mountain
let	cut

Name _____  Unit 29

Write the Words

Directions: Write the words in the spaces.

far, Indian, real, almost, let, above, girl, sometimes, mountain, cut

1. far _____

6. above _____

_____

_____

2. Indian _____

7. girl _____

_____

_____

3. real _____

8. sometimes _____

_____

_____

4. almost _____

9. mountain _____

_____

_____

5. let _____

10. cut _____

_____

_____

Name _____

Find the Words—Level A

Directions: There are 10 Instant Words hidden here. Can you find and circle them?

Here are the words to look for:

above, cut, girl, let, real, almost, far, Indian, mountain, sometimes

Q D L Z I Z V Y H J M K
G X B P M A B O V E M M
H I N D I A N F A R Z L
A G L E T U X R L Y E P
M C T H M Y H U N Q O H
P O K P Y H D N N S V A
H U R E A L M O S T C A
R U T H C U T Q V U Y E
M R V B Y X L A C F Q J
S L I E K G R M A R H R
T K G S O M E T I M E S
G I R L M O U N T A I N

Write the Words in Sentences

Directions: Choose a word from the word box to complete each sentence and write the word in the space.

Indian, let, above, girl, cut, far, real, almost, sometimes, mountain

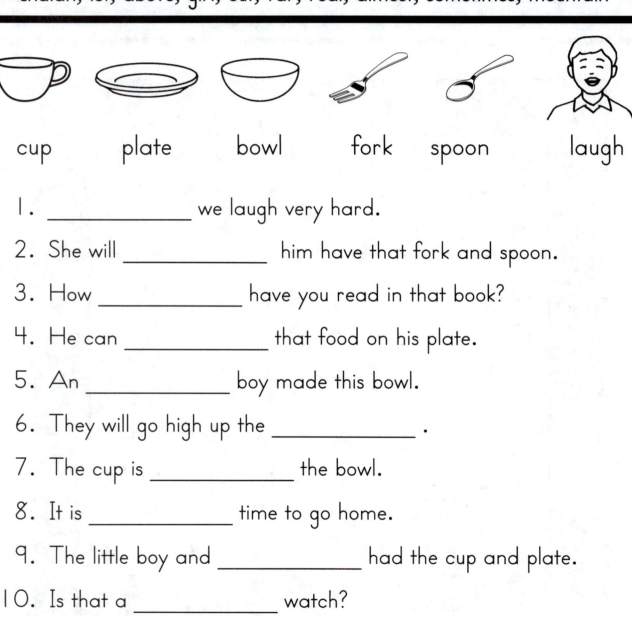

cup   plate   bowl   fork   spoon   laugh

1. _____ we laugh very hard.

2. She will _____ him have that fork and spoon.

3. How _____ have you read in that book?

4. He can _____ that food on his plate.

5. An _____ boy made this bowl.

6. They will go high up the _____ .

7. The cup is _____ the bowl.

8. It is _____ time to go home.

9. The little boy and _____ had the cup and plate.

10. Is that a _____ watch?

Name _____

Find the Words—Level B

Directions: There are 10 Instant Words hidden here. Can you find and circle them?

Here are the words to look for:

| above, cut, girl, let, real, almost, far, Indian, mountain, sometimes |

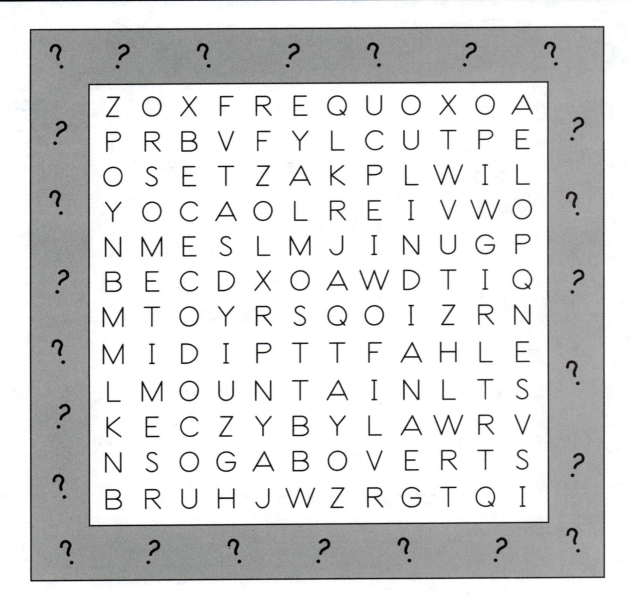

```
Z O X F R E Q U O X O A
P R B V F Y L C U T P E
O S E T Z A K P L W I L
Y O C A O L R E I V W O
N M E S L M J I N U G P
B E C D X O A W D T I Q
M T O Y R S Q O I Z R N
M I D I P T T F A H L E
L M O U N T A I N L T S
K E C Z Y B Y L A W R V
N S O G A B O V E R T S
B R U H J W Z R G T Q I
```

Choose the Correct Words

Directions: Choose the correct word to complete each sentence and write the word in the space.

far, Indian, real, almost, let, above, girl, sometimes, mountain, cut

laugh   cup   plate   bowl   fork   spoon

1. She _____ left her spoon in her bowl.
   above almost girl

2. The little boy can _____ use a fork.
   let cut sometimes

3. Did you hear the _____ laugh?
   mountain girl almost

4. These men have run very _____ .
   sometimes far Indian

5. How far is it up that _____ ?
   above mountain real

6. Put the cup _____ the plate.
   far girl above

7. We can hear the _____ children laugh.
   Indian let almost

8. It is hard to _____ through that.
   far real cut

9. Are those his _____ feet?
   Indian real sometimes

10. I will not _____ him get too far away.
    let cut mountain

Just-for-Fun Mystery Words

Be a detective! Can you use the code symbols to solve the mystery words?

Directions: Look at the code symbols under each line. Match each symbol to each letter and fill in the letters on each line. Check the words that you made to make sure they match the instant words in the box.

far, Indian, real, almost, let, above, girl, sometimes, mountain, cut

1. ___ ___ ___ ___ ___ ___ ___ ___ ___
  ♡ ● ♥ □ ⊠ ✕ ♥ □ ♡

6. ___ ___ ___ ___ ___ ___ ___ ___
  ♥ ● ▲ → ⊠ ✳ ✕ →

2. ___ ___ ___
  ☆ □ ⊠

7. ___ ___ ___ ___ ___ ___
  ✕ → ÷ ✕ ✳ →

3. ___ ___ ___ ___
  ▼ ✕ ■ ☆

8. ___ ___ ___ ___ ___
  ✳ △ ● + □

4. ___ ___ ___ ___
  ■ □ ✳ ☆

9. ___ ___ ___ ___ ___ ___
  ✳ ☆ ♥ ● ♡ ⊠

5. ___ ___ ___
  ↑ ▲ ⊠

10. ___ ___ ___
  ↓ ✳ ■

Code Symbols

a = ✳ b = △ c = ↑ d = ÷ e = □ f = ↓ g = ▼ h = ⊙ i = ✕

j = ○ k = ▽ l = ☆ m = ♥ n = → o = ● p = ▫ q = ← r = ■

s = ♡ t = ⊠ u = ▲ v = + w = ◮ x = ❀ y = ★ z = ⊗

                   #3503 Instant Word Practice Book

Flashcards

Directions: Cut out the flashcards and use them to help you learn the words.

young, talk, soon, list, song, leave, family, body, music, color

young	leave
talk	family
soon	body
list	music
song	color

Name _____  Unit 30

Write the Words

Directions: Write the words in the spaces.

young, talk, soon, list, song, leave, family, body, music, color

1. young _____

6. leave _____

_____

_____

2. talk _____

7. family _____

_____

_____

3. soon _____

8. body _____

_____

_____

4. list _____

9. music _____

_____

_____

5. song _____

10. color _____

_____

_____

Name _____

Find the Words—Level A

Directions: There are 10 Instant Words hidden here. Can you find and circle them?

Here are the words to look for:

body, family, list, song, talk, color, leave, music, soon, young

```
B O D Y S O N G H
O M U S I C M E N
A Z Y F O G Y F W
O A H J K K T V W
A C O L O R Y H G
U T W F A M I L Y
M O Y O U N G W Q
T A L K S O O N P
L E A V E L I S T
```

Name _____  Unit 30

Write the Words in Sentences

Directions: Choose a word from the word box to complete each sentence and write the word in the space.

| song, leave, family, music, color, young, talk, soon, list, body |

store   gas station   church   theater   barn   sing

1. She went to the store with her _____ .

2. They will learn a new _____ in church.

3. What _____ is that barn?

4. Don't _____ while people sing.

5. His feet are too big for his _____ .

6. They will go to the theater after they _____ the gas station.

7. Is he _____ or old?

8. People play _____ at this theater.

9. He said they would come see us very _____ .

10. They will make a _____ of what they need.

Name _____  Unit 30

Find the Words—Level B

Directions: There are 10 Instant Words hidden here. Can you find and circle them?

Here are the words to look for:

body, family, list, song, talk, color, leave, music, soon, young

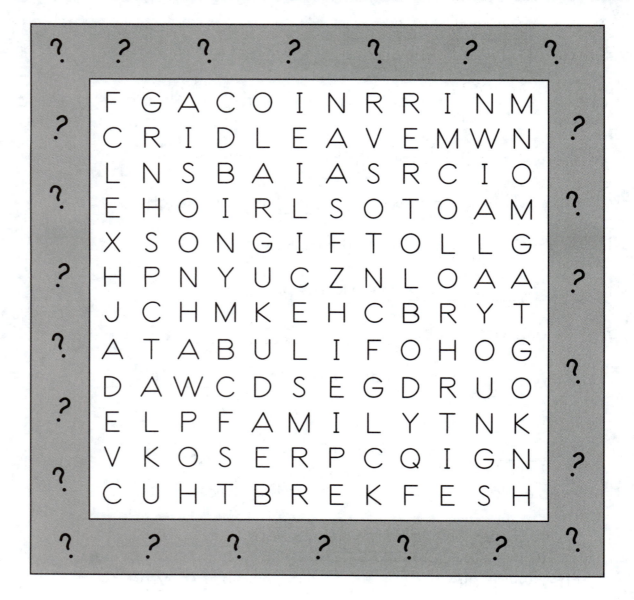

Choose the Correct Words

Choose the correct word to complete each sentence and write the word in the space.

young, talk, soon, list, song, leave, family, body, music, color

sing   store   gas station   church   theater   barn

1. At the gas station they will work on the _____ of our car.
   song family body

2. The girl will sing a _____ at her church.
   song family list

3. There is a _____ boy at the barn.
   music body young

4. Don't _____ in the theater.
   song talk young

5. What kind of _____ does he sing?
   leave music color

6. We need to go to the store _____ .
   talk soon body

7. What did he write on his _____ ?
   list soon color

8. They like to sing with their _____ .
   talk leave family

9. What _____ is the mountain?
   music young color

10. They don't want to _____ now.
    leave soon list

Name _____

Unit 30

Just-for-Fun Letter Squares

Directions: Write the missing letters in the squares to spell the words from the word box. Then copy the completed words on the lines below the squares.

young, talk, soon, list, song, leave, family, body, music, color

1. | t | | | |

_____

2. | s | | | g |

_____

3. | | e | a | | |

_____

4. | | | | i | c |

_____

5. | y | | | | |

_____

6. | b | | | y |

_____

7. | | o | o | |

_____

8. | | | s | t |

_____

9. | | | | | l | y |

_____

10. | c | | | | |

_____

Unit 1 Answer Key

35. Find the Words A

```
N   F   H   Y   I   J  (A)
Z   N  (I   T)  B   L   Q
(I   N) D   J  (T   H   E)
(O   F) T  (Y   O   U)  H
(T   H   A   T)(A   N   D)
X   R   S  (T   O)(I   S)
B   C   S   O   K   L   Z
```

36. Match Sentences with Pictures

1. b
2. f
3. d
4. a
5. c
6. e

37. Find the Words B

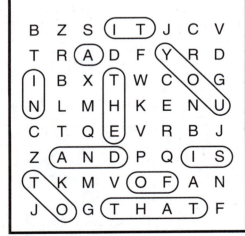

38. Choose the Correct Words

1. that
2. and
3. the
4. of
5. you
6. in

39. Just-for-Fun Word Scramble

1. is
2. that
3. the
4. it
5. a
6. of
7. and
8. in
9. you
10. to

Unit 2 Answer Key

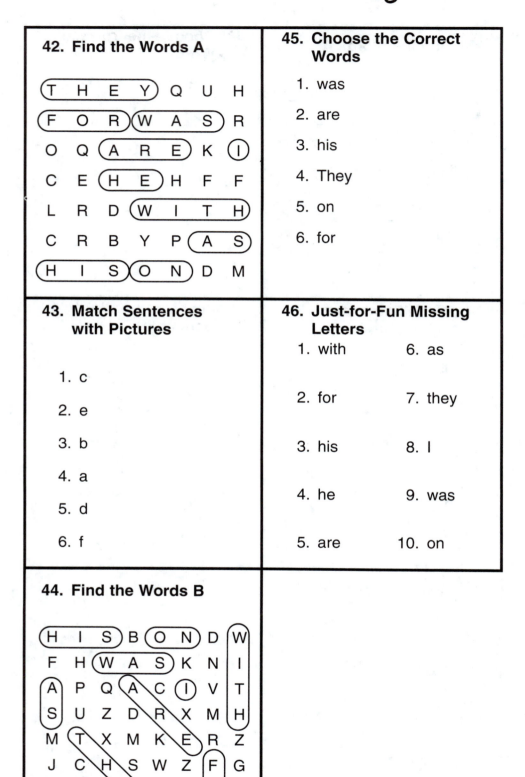

42. Find the Words A

T H E Y Q U H
F O R W A S R
O Q A R E K I
C E H E H F F
L R D W I T H
C R B Y P A S
H I S O N D M

43. Match Sentences with Pictures

1. c
2. e
3. b
4. a
5. d
6. f

44. Find the Words B

H I S B O N D W
F H W A S K N I
A P Q A C I V T
S U Z D R X M H
M T X M K E R Z
J C H S W Z F G
H E Q E R H O B
L T R D Y L R S

45. Choose the Correct Words

1. was
2. are
3. his
4. They
5. on
6. for

46. Just-for-Fun Missing Letters

1. with   6. as

2. for   7. they

3. his   8. I

4. he   9. was

5. are   10. on

Unit 3 Answer Key

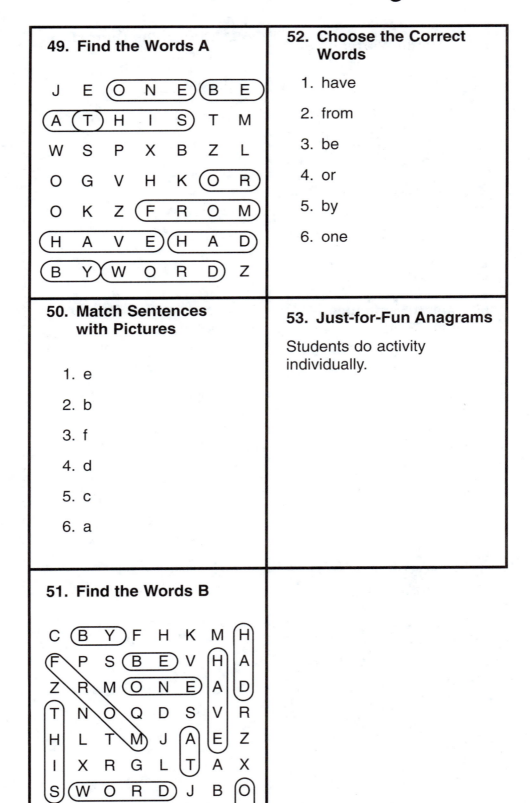

49. Find the Words A

```
J  E  O  N  E  B  E
A  T  H  I  S  T  M
W  S  P  X  B  Z  L
O  G  V  H  K  O  R
O  K  Z  F  R  O  M
H  A  V  E  H  A  D
B  Y  W  O  R  D  Z
```

52. Choose the Correct Words

1. have
2. from
3. be
4. or
5. by
6. one

50. Match Sentences with Pictures

1. e
2. b
3. f
4. d
5. c
6. a

53. Just-for-Fun Anagrams

Students do activity individually.

51. Find the Words B

```
C  B  Y  F  H  K  M  H
F  P  S  B  E  V  H  A
Z  R  M  O  N  E  A  D
T  N  O  Q  D  S  V  R
H  L  T  M  J  A  E  Z
I  X  R  G  L  T  A  X
S  W  O  R  D  J  B  O
E  T  W  I  N  X  C  R
```

Unit 4 Answer Key

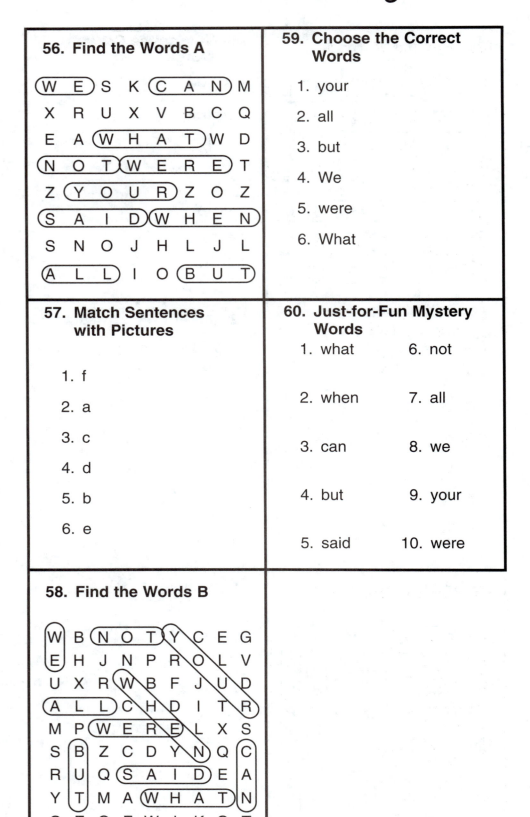

56. Find the Words A

```
W E  S  K  C A N  M
X  R  U  X  V  B  C  Q
E  A  W H A T  W  D
N  O T W E R E  T
Z  Y O U R  Z  O  Z
S A I D W H E N
S  N  O  J  H  L  J  L
A L L  I  O  B U T
```

57. Match Sentences with Pictures

1. f
2. a
3. c
4. d
5. b
6. e

58. Find the Words B

```
W  B  N O T Y  C  E  G
E  H  J  N  P  R O L  V
U  X  R  W B  F  J  U D
A L L  C  H  D  I  T  R
M  P  W E R E  L  X  S
S  B  Z  C  D  Y  N  Q  C
R  U  Q  S A I D  E  A
Y  T  M  A  W H A T  N
O  Z  Q  F  W  I  K  O  T
```

59. Choose the Correct Words

1. your
2. all
3. but
4. We
5. were
6. What

60. Just-for-Fun Mystery Words

1. what   6. not

2. when   7. all

3. can   8. we

4. but   9. your

5. said   10. were

Unit 5 Answer Key

63. Find the Words A

```
L (T H E R E) W X
R C J (H O W) U I
L X P (W H I C H)
G E Q (U S E) W W
(S H E) K H M A O
U F C X V A (A N)
(T H E I R) (I F) V
(D O) L (E A C H) I
```

66. Choose the Correct Words

1. their
2. Which
3. She
4. Each
5. do
6. How

64. Match Sentences with Pictures

1. d
2. c
3. e
4. b
5. a
6. f

67. Just-for-Fun Letter Squares

1. their   6. each
2. she   7. use
3. an   8. do
4. which   9. if
5. there   10. how

65. Find the Words B

```
C G I (H O W) J (A D
K (T H E I R) L H N)
(W M (D O) O Q (T T (U
V H E Z S O H P S
Y E (I F) D M E H E)
B C L (C W L R) X Q
E D N J H) A E) S U
N U W Q B P T R N
(S H E) I (E A C H) F
```

Unit 6 Answer Key

70. Find the Words A

```
U  P  Y  R  M  R  S  O
E  J  C  A  T  H  E  M
H  N  P  Y  J  L  U  O
P  O  T  H  E  R  C  N
L  E  A  B  O  U  T  E
U  D  J  T  H  E  S  E
M  A  N  Y  T  H  E  N
W  I  L  L  O  U  T  N
```

73. Choose the Correct Words

1. about
2. These
3. them
4. Many
5. so
6. other

71. Match Sentences with Pictures

1. b
2. d
3. e
4. c
5. a
6. f

74. Just-for-Fun Word Scramble

1. many
2. so
3. other
4. will
5. out

6. them
7. about
8. then
9. up
10. these

72. Find the Words B

```
M  C  E  G  O  K  D  M  F
J  A  L  P  T  W  O  R  V
T  O  N  Q  H  I  J  U  P
Z  H  Q  Y  E  L  I  B  T
U  B  E  H  R  L  X  L  N
T  T  V  S  J  T  H  E  M
R  H  W  D  E  P  X  N  S
P  E  N  L  Z  R  O  S  O
T  N  Y  A  B  O  U  T  B
```

Unit 7 Answer Key

77. Find the Words A

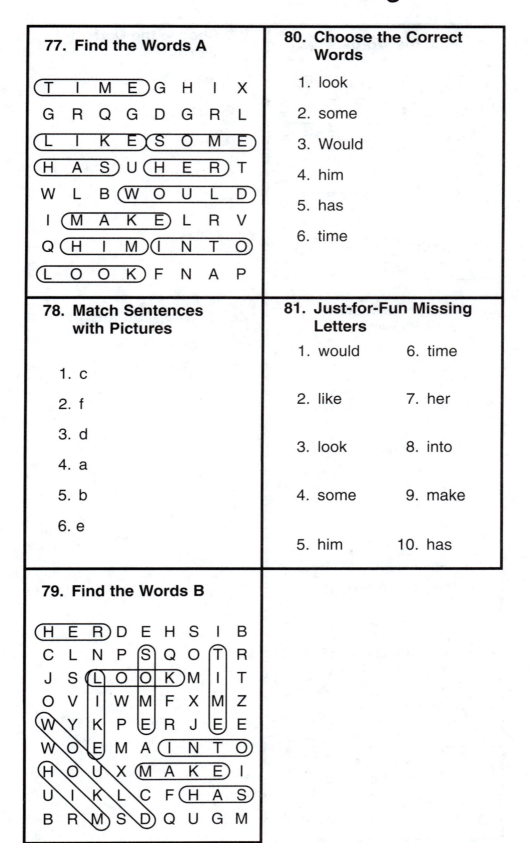

```
T I M E G H I X
G R Q G D G R L
L I K E S O M E
H A S U H E R T
W L B W O U L D
I M A K E L R V
Q H I M I N T O
L O O K F N A P
```

78. Match Sentences with Pictures

1. c
2. f
3. d
4. a
5. b
6. e

79. Find the Words B

```
H E R D E H S I B
C L N P S Q O T R
J S L O O K M I T
O V I W M F X M Z
W Y K P E R J E E
W O E M A I N T O
H O U X M A K E I
U I K L C F H A S
B R M S D Q U G M
```

80. Choose the Correct Words

1. look
2. some
3. Would
4. him
5. has
6. time

81. Just-for-Fun Missing Letters

1. would
2. like
3. look
4. some
5. him

6. time
7. her
8. into
9. make
10. has

Unit 8 Answer Key

84. Find the Words A

```
T W O  J  O  W A Y  F
H  N U M B E R  A  Q
H  P E O P L E  G O
K  K  O  F  L  L  C  V  R
N O  F  C  W  S  T  E  L
X  U  R  J  D  S E E  U
C  W  I  N  N  X  L  R  G
Y  K  X  W R I T E  D
M O R E C O U L D
```

85. Match Sentences with Pictures

1. e
2. d
3. b
4. f
5. a
6. c

87. Choose the Correct Words

1. write
2. more
3. way
4. number
5. go
6. see

88. Just-for-Fun Anagrams

Students do activity individually.

86. Find the Words B

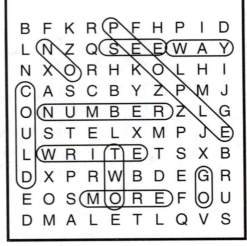

```
B  F  K  R  P  F  H  P  I  D
L  N  Z  Q  S E E W A Y
N  X  O  R  H  K  O  L  H  I
C  A  S  C  B  Y  Z  P  M  J
O  N U M B E R  Z  L  G
U  S  T  E  L  X  M  P  J  E
L  W R I T E  T  S  X  B
D  X  P  R  W  B  D  E  G  R
E  O  S  M O R E  F  O  U
D  M  A  L  E  T  L  Q  V  S
```

Unit 9 Answer Key

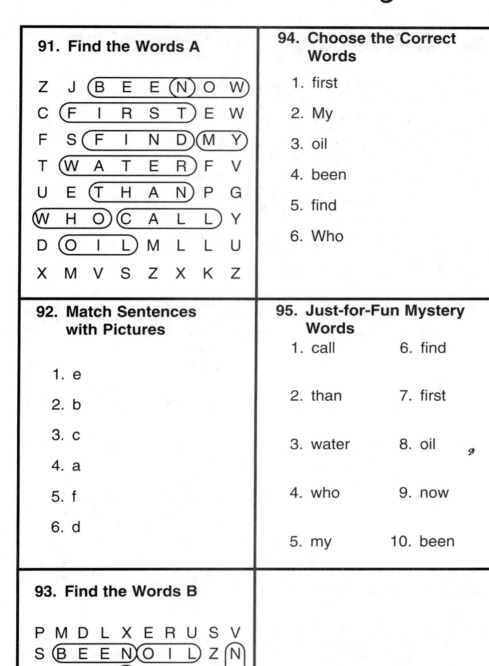

91. Find the Words A

```
Z  J  B  E  E  N  O  W
C  F  I  R  S  T  E  W
F  S  F  I  N  D  M  Y
T  W  A  T  E  R  F  V
U  E  T  H  A  N  P  G
W  H  O  C  A  L  L  Y
D  O  I  L  M  L  L  U
X  M  V  S  Z  X  K  Z
```

92. Match Sentences with Pictures

1. e
2. b
3. c
4. a
5. f
6. d

93. Find the Words B

```
P  M  D  L  X  E  R  U  S  V
S  B  E  E  N  O  I  L  Z  N
R  C  W  P  F  T  E  R  G  O
T  H  A  N  I  D  M  X  Q  W
K  X  L  F  R  E  Y  P  F  Y
H  W  R  M  S  F  Q  U  I  S
U  S  A  N  T  A  T  I  N  J
R  J  L  T  Q  J  B  A  D  F
C  A  L  L  E  Q  V  E  Z  H
Q  W  N  Y  P  R  C  W  H  O
```

94. Choose the Correct Words

1. first
2. My
3. oil
4. been
5. find
6. Who

95. Just-for-Fun Mystery Words

1. call
2. than
3. water
4. who
5. my
6. find
7. first
8. oil
9. now
10. been

Unit 10 Answer Key

98. Find the Words A

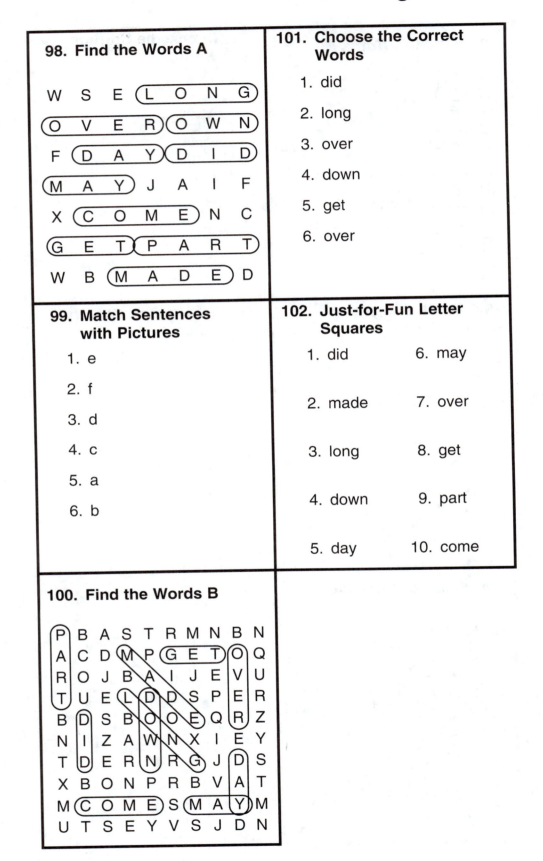

99. Match Sentences with Pictures

1. e
2. f
3. d
4. c
5. a
6. b

100. Find the Words B

101. Choose the Correct Words

1. did
2. long
3. over
4. down
5. get
6. over

102. Just-for-Fun Letter Squares

1. did
2. made
3. long
4. down
5. day
6. may
7. over
8. get
9. part
10. come

Unit 11 Answer Key

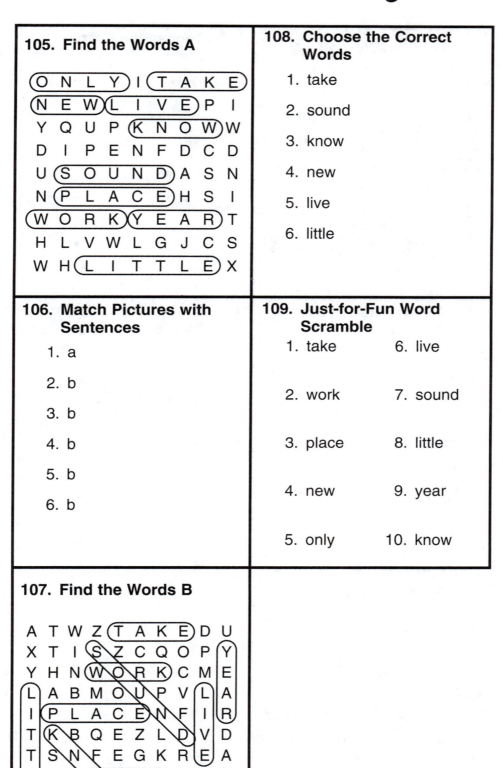

105. Find the Words A

```
O N L Y  I  T A K E
N E W L  I  V E P  I
Y Q U P K N O W W
D  I  P E N F D C D
U S O U N D A S N
N P L A C E H S  I
W O R K Y E A R T
H L V W L G J C S
W H L  I  T T L E X
```

108. Choose the Correct Words

1. take
2. sound
3. know
4. new
5. live
6. little

106. Match Pictures with Sentences

1. a
2. b
3. b
4. b
5. b
6. b

109. Just-for-Fun Word Scramble

1. take   6. live
2. work   7. sound
3. place   8. little
4. new   9. year
5. only   10. know

107. Find the Words B

```
A T W Z T A K E D U
X T  I  S Z C Q O P Y
Y H N W O R K C M E
L A B M O U P V L A
I  P L A C E N F  I  R
T K B Q E Z L D V D
T S N F E G K R E A
L G U O N L Y S Z L
E R J V W Y N E W B
H W T  I  X J C D K E
```

Unit 12 Answer Key

112. Find the Words A

```
B  E  Y  W  A  S  V  Z
T  X  U  P  H  O  M  U
O  U  R  T  H  I  N  G
B  A  C  K  G  I  V  E
K  A  F  T  E  R  M  E
T  I  M  O  S  T  S  V
J  U  S  T  N  A  M  E
X  V  E  R  Y  E  N  W
```

115. Choose the Correct Words

1. after
2. most
3. very
4. name
5. give
6. Our

113. Match Pictures with Sentences

1. a
2. b
3. a
4. b
5. b
6. a

116. Just-for-Fun Missing Words

1. back
2. most
3. thing
4. me
5. our

6. name
7. give
8. after
9. just
10. very

114. Find the Words B

```
A  U  N  J  K  L  E  S  F  A
C  T  P  A  O  B  A  C  K  H
V  H  B  W  M  V  G  M  K  V
L  I  T  J  D  E  F  J  Q  E
W  N  C  G  N  X  M  U  G  R
D  G  Q  R  I  Z  E  S  I  Y
K  X  M  J  D  V  Y  T  H  U
Y  M  O  S  T  Z  E  G  I  P
F  A  F  T  E  R  I  O  U  R
R  Z  B  H  C  S  N  T  O  B
```

Unit 13 Answer Key

119. Find the Words A

```
U J H O G M I A P K X
X Q G F D Y C R J E Y
V B E S N S R Z E X B
E G R E A T M A N X Z
S A Y T H R O U G H R
M U C H Q G O O D B U
S E N T E N C E B M H
H E L P N W H E R E A
U C W B I I A M M H M
I T H I N K T Q S C T
Z V W F L D U E B A W
```

122. Choose the Correct Words

1. Where
2. through
3. sentence
4. much
5. great
6. say

120. Match Pictures with Sentences

1. a
2. b
3. a
4. b
5. a
6. b

123. Just-for-Fun Anagrams

Students do activity individually.

121. Find the Words B

```
A C B M L C A M E Z
W H E R E K B U C D
H J R H E L P C E T
E B S G R S F H I H
Z G S K T H I N K R
G Y R N E A S R V O
O X O E J V A J E U
O I D M A N Y S E G
D W P U M T Q R S H
V S E N T E N C E T
```

Unit 14 Answer Key

126. Find the Words A

```
O  L  D  C  S  A  M  E  E
A  N  Y  F  A  M  E  A  N
B  O  Y  V  E  R  T  O  O
K  B  G  V  F  L  I  N  E
E  T  C  Y  V  V  Y  K  Z
B  F  C  A  I  I  L  P  S
Y  E  T  E  L  L  O  Q  K
O  R  I  G  H  T  P  T  R
V  Y  L  B  E  F  O  R  E
```

127. Match Pictures with Sentences

1. a
2. b
3. a
4. a
5. b
6. a

128. Find the Words B

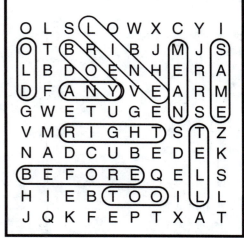

```
O  L  S  L  O  W  X  C  Y  I
O  T  B  R  I  B  J  M  J  S
L  B  D  O  E  N  H  E  R  A
D  F  A  N  Y  V  E  A  R  M
G  W  E  T  U  G  E  N  S  E
V  M  R  I  G  H  T  S  T  Z
N  A  D  C  U  B  E  D  E  K
B  E  F  O  R  E  Q  E  L  S
H  I  E  B  T  O  O  I  L  L
J  Q  K  F  E  P  T  X  A  T
```

129. Choose the Correct Words

1. before
2. right
3. same
4. too
5. mean
6. old

130. Just-for-Fun Mystery Words

1. boy
2. same
3. too
4. before
5. old
6. tell
7. mean
8. any
9. right
10. line

Unit 15 Answer Key

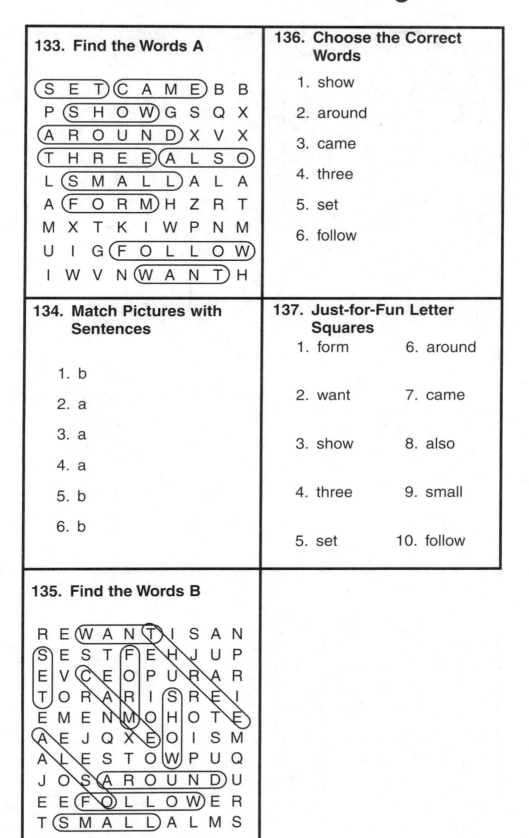

133. Find the Words A

```
S E T  C A M E  B  B
P  S H O W  G  S  Q  X
A R O U N D  X  V  X
T H R E E  A L S O
L  S M A L L  A  L  A
A  F O R M  H  Z  R  T
M  X  T  K  I  W  P  N  M
U  I  G  F O L L O W
I  W  V  N  W A N T  H
```

136. Choose the Correct Words

1. show
2. around
3. came
4. three
5. set
6. follow

134. Match Pictures with Sentences

1. b
2. a
3. a
4. a
5. b
6. b

137. Just-for-Fun Letter Squares

1. form   6. around

2. want   7. came

3. show   8. also

4. three   9. small

5. set   10. follow

135. Find the Words B

```
R E  W A N T  I  S A N
S E S T  F E H J U P
E V  C E O P U R A R
T O R A R I  S R E I
E M E N M O H O T E
A E J Q X E O I S M
A L E S T O W P U Q
J O S A R O U N D  U
E E F O L L O W E R
T S M A L L  A L M S
```

Unit 16 Answer Key

140. Find the Words A

```
A N O T H E R  J Z P
G Z U W H S W K E R
L A R G E M U S T  B
U H N C P U T E Z H
R O A Q H Z V I C S
A E U F O V D O E S
B I G X W E L L S C
G O H S K E V E N D
W X S U C H M G Q C
U X C O T X D P H A
```

143. Choose the Correct Words

1. large
2. another
3. end
4. such
5. does
6. must

141. Match Pictures with Sentences

1. a
2. a
3. b
4. a
5. b
6. b

144. Just-for-Fun Word Scramble

1. must   6. another

2. well   7. large

3. such   8. put

4. does   9. big

5. even   10. end

142. Find the Words B

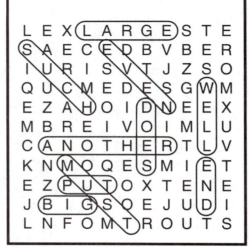

```
L E X L A R G E S T E
S A E C E D B V B E R
I U R I S V T J Z S O
Q U C M E D S G W M
E Z A H O I D N E E X
M B R E I V O I M L U
C A N O T H E R T L V
K N M O Q E S M I E T
E Z P U T O X T E N E
J B I G S O E J U D I
L N F O M T R O U T S
```

Unit 17 Answer Key

147. Find the Words A

```
D B E C A U S E R R
Y C T U R N E E D O
J O X N M E N C T O
H Y L A N D J D H L
R E F X Q M R O H G
I L K P D G C N P L
X P B E A S K T R S
T U Z N P A V Y L C
X W H Y N L H E R E
R E A D M W E N T F
```

150. Choose the Correct Words

1. turn

2. because

3. read

4. land

5. need

6. Ask

148. Match Pictures with Sentences

1. b

2. a

3. b

4. a

5. a

6. a

151. Just-for-Fun Missing Letters

1. read   6. ask

2. land   7. turn

3. because   8. went

4. here   9. need

5. men   10. why

149. Find the Words B

```
V E O J I W S T N P X
N Z N H E R E N I M E
A I J E Q O Z Q A Z D
E S B E C A U S E N R
Q U K L O P E N W H Y
P M E N X R U V S M E
S E R J O W E N T U T
A L A N D E R A R O U
S Z R T C A X K D D R
R E N E E D Z L Y S N
U X C O D M V J K L J
```

Unit 18 Answer Key

4. Find the Words A

```
T E L V G B M O V E Q O
Q G Y T S I I P K I A O
O D I F F E R E N T L S
P I C T U R E T R Y Z N
W Y T F W L Y E T E K O
C X P R W M B J A Z W X
R R N V G I S B H K E A
S B M X C H A N G E U S
Q I W D D M W H O M E P
F E O A G A I N K I N D
J V D P Q H A N D O J R
O K Z L Y D H R H N N G
```

157. Choose the Correct Words

1. different

2. kind

3. try

4. change

5. move

6. hand

155. Match Pictures with Sentences

1. a

2. a

3. a

4. a

5. b

6. b

158. Just-for-Fun Anagrams

Students do activity individually.

156. Find the Words B

```
O H I S T R U M E R N
Z I O G C H A N G E E
U H F M P I C T U R E
S J X K E N Q U X E P
E Q D I F F E R E N T
Z V M U B M W Z D O R
H O Y O T K I N D N Y
I A D L V F Q U R P O
A B N C S E N C Y B S
O S U D T E A G A I N
E F G O P E R G O N T
```

Unit 19 Answer Key

161. Find the Words A

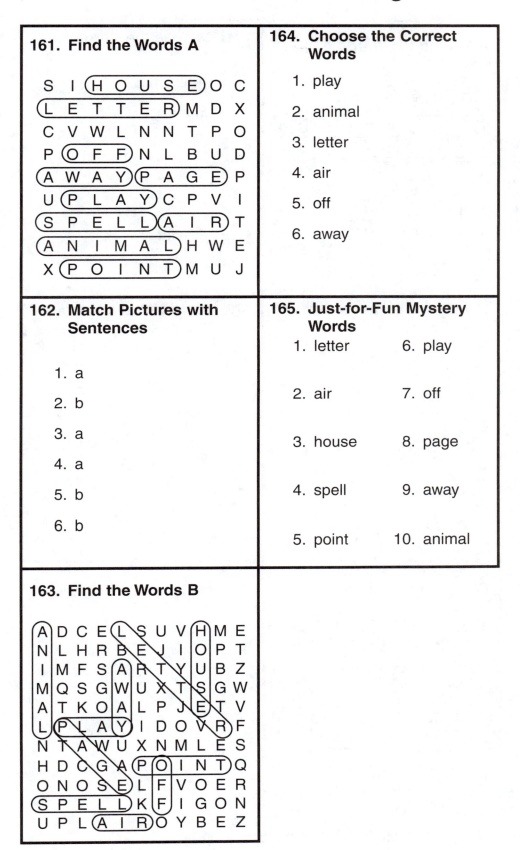

```
S  I  H O U S E  O  C
L E T T E R  M  D  X
C  V  W  L  N  N  T  P  O
P  O F F  N  L  B  U  D
A W A Y  P A G E  P
U  P L A Y  C  P  V  I
S P E L L  A I R  T
A N I M A L  H  W  E
X  P O I N T  M  U  J
```

164. Choose the Correct Words

1. play

2. animal

3. letter

4. air

5. off

6. away

162. Match Pictures with Sentences

1. a

2. b

3. a

4. a

5. b

6. b

165. Just-for-Fun Mystery Words

1. letter   6. play

2. air   7. off

3. house   8. page

4. spell   9. away

5. point   10. animal

163. Find the Words B

```
A D C E L S U V H M E
N L H R B E J I O P T
I M F S A R T Y U B Z
M Q S G W U X T S G W
A T K O A L P J E T V
L P L A Y I D O V R F
N T A W U X N M L E S
H D C G A P O I N T Q
O N O S E L F V O E R
S P E L L K F I G O N
U P L A I R O Y B E Z
```

Unit 20 Answer Key

68. Find the Words A

```
D A M E R I C A R R
Y M O T H E R C O J
O X N C F O U N D T
S T U D Y S T I L L
L E A R N O H Y J D
H L R E F X Q M R O
H G I W O R L D L K
P D G C N P L X P B
H I G H A N S W E R
E T R S S H O U L D
```

171. Choose the Correct Words

1. America
2. found
3. world
4. should
5. study
6. answer

169. Match Pictures with Sentences

1. b
2. a
3. a
4. a
5. a
6. a

172. Just-for-Fun Letter Squares

1. found   6. high

2. still   7. answer

3. mother   8. learn

4. study   9. world

5. should   10. America

170. Find the Words B

```
E L F O N S E N B O G
R A E R N E H I G H V
S M E A S O A O E F A
T K I H R D M B U C P
I N G O K N E S A L C
L F O U N D R V N B D
L C J R D L I U S J E
S T U D Y Q C T W E M
O I K E X J A N E B O
X O S M O T H E R T S
Z N A P T O W O R L D
```

Unit 21 Answer Key

175. Find the Words A

```
L A S T U O E L M I
B E T W E E N D S P
Q B U L D P L A N T
T V R O W N A R M U
N E A R B E L O W A
A U Q A D D J I R B
F O O D E V E R Y Q
U T E L V G B Q O Q
G Y T S I I P K I A
O C O U N T R Y O L
```

178. Choose the Correct Words

1. near
2. every
3. add
4. own
5. between
6. food
7. last
8. plant
9. country
10. below

176. Write the Words in Sentences

1. every
2. between or below or near
3. food or plant
4. own
5. plant
6. last
7. add
8. near or below
9. country
10. near or below

179. Just-for-Fun Word Scramble

1. plant
2. own
3. add
4. food
5. below
6. every
7. between
8. last
9. country
10. near

177. Find the Words B

```
F E T F S Y N J C A W O
O C G M R N P E K I L X
P O S F E R G Q A J A D
E U T Z O D H H G R S O
A N O I J O O M P D T L
Q T Q I N K D F L X N Y
F R U V A D D W A O E C
R Y U G M E L K N L W Z
B E L O W X V Y T C R N
S L B E T W E E N B H J
D H I A P Q B Z R M K A
P C T B V U F N V Y B W
```

Unit 22 Answer Key

2. Find the Words A

```
C N E V E R J C W
O A L I G H T E U
K J Y S C H O O L
S F A T H E R W V
C I T Y T R E E F
V O E Y E F D M X
Q R D R S F D D D
K E E P S T A R T
L L L E A R T H K
```

185. Choose the Correct Words

1. start	6. eye
2. earth	7. school
3. light	8. never
4. father	9. city
5. tree	10. keep

183. Write the Words in Sentences

1. start	6. earth
2. keep	7. city
3. school	8. light
4. tree	9. eye
5. father or school or tree	10. never

186. Just-for-Fun Missing Letters

1. school	6. father
2. never	7. earth
3. start	8. tree
4. eye	9. light
5. keep	10. city

184. Find the Words B

```
X K J E Y E Y S K O N L
F R E S T A W L E G E O
Y Q E E U Q V J A S V C
G F B C P B P O R I E C
Z J A E L I G H T Y R S
C C D T D N I M H S E U
I A H Q H Z A V N M T L
T S I H Y E S E Z R R G
Y K Y S T A R T D O E T
D E K O Y N D O W R E G
B A O S C H O O L F S B
T E C C Q H U I J K O V
```

Unit 23 Answer Key

189. Find the Words A

```
G M Y (S A W) G O P F
D E V O B A W P K M
Q Q A J R Y (D O N T)
O P G D W V J (F E W)
I G B J C C I E K S
G P N (U N D E R) Q J
W R M (S T O R Y) B W
B A (W H I L E) M I W
(L E F (T) H O U G H T)
(A L O N G) (H E A D) E
```

192. Choose the Correct Words

1. thought
2. head
3. under
4. along
5. Don't
6. story
7. few
8. while
9. saw
10. left

190. Write the Words in Sentences

1. story
2. left
3. saw
4. along
5. few
6. while
7. head
8. Don't
9. under
10. thought

193. Just-for-Fun Anagrams

Students do activity individually.

191. Find the Words B

```
K Z A P M B C Y Q B Z A
R W P L B A (L G I S (T H
(D O N T) C (F L E K Q (H J
E D S I J E C R F P O B
A E T D U W (S Y S T U C
Q H R G I B Z A G O G U
P (A L O N G) B A W O H U
(U N F H M V L M W N T) L
N O F (H J K (S T O R Y) Z
D J C (L E S A M U E D T
E B P G E A N (W H I L E)
(R) H M O L S D) F M N H G
```

Unit 24 Answer Key

Find the Words A

```
L M I G H T Y A S E E M
S L I F E C L O S E R P
B E G I N M V E D F E K
H A R D X W H B L F P B
M P J S O M E T H I N G
B O P E N E X T N X J B
F C D Z D S C N U F L K
O A E X A M P L E O H M
S A S Q Z C B D Z F L J
F Z H S K N B Y Z L B L
E D M A D Y W I H N H B
X R E V J Q E X A I K P
```

199. Choose the Correct Words

1. might
2. something
3. seem
4. open
5. hard
6. life
7. next
8. example
9. begin
10. close

197. Write the Words in Sentences

1. something
2. seem
3. next
4. begin
5. hard
6. example
7. life
8. close or open or begin
9. open
10. might

200. Just-for-Fun Mystery Words

1. something
2. life
3. seem
4. open
5. example
6. begin
7. might
8. close
9. hard
10. next

198. Find the Words B

```
Y N E X T Y O R J P E W
L E M U S O P E N A U M
E U N I O E G X R S C I
N B O T G S Q A W O W J
W Y B H E H J M O M A G
T H B V C O T P P E T R
F J A W J S Z L A T C G
S L A R J A D E W H J S
E J N U D O B E G I N T
E L M O H M A T I N K R
M C L O S E D E V G I Z
M Q D B R Y T L I F E H
```

Unit 25 Answer Key

203. Find the Words A

```
D I M P O R T A N T R R
Y T O G E T H E R U N C
G R O U P O J O X N C T
O H Y J D H L R E F X Q
M R O F T E N O H G I L
K P D G C N P L X P B E
T R S T U Z N P A V Y L
C X N L M G O T F B B E
J B V L Q M Y A X J R B
A N D M Q I U F A L K Y
E B O T H G A L W A Y S
P A P E R Q T H O S E Q
```

206. Choose the Correct Words

1. together
2. often
3. important
4. run
5. paper
6. got
7. always
8. both
9. those
10. group

204. Write the Words in Sentences

1. run
2. got
3. important
4. often or together or always
5. group
6. both
7. always or often
8. together
9. paper
10. those

207. Just-for-Fun Letter Squares

1. both
2. those
3. got
4. always
5. group
6. run
7. paper
8. often
9. together
10. important

205. Find the Words B

```
W R M B R O N C E B E T
G I A N I G O T W B F O
A S M A C M I W B V E G
L O H P T U T H O S E E
W P J M O E U P T E I T
A T O K M R A L H S R H
Y O S G B T T P X Y O E
S Y Q U E O E A D I F R
F G R O U P Q P N C T A
Z G P J K I L E M T E B
H I R U N G H R N O N K
C O D E E F Z I U Y J P
```

Unit 26 Answer Key

Find the Words A

```
C A R Q I W W H I T E
D D M W P F E O J V D
P Q O J R O K Z L Y D
N I G H T D F E E T M
W A L K H M I L E R H
N N G R S S Y G P O D
C H I L D R E N S E A
X W K D U N T I L M L
V H P J K D T H E G L
K F B P O S I D E T W
N A U A O L Y Q H W X
```

213. Choose the Correct Words

1. walk
6. side

2. sea
7. feet

3. white
8. until

4. car
9. night

5. children
10. mile

211. Write the Words in Sentences

1. walk
6. until

2. car
7. side

3. white
8. night

4. sea
9. feet

5. mile
10. children

214. Just-for-Fun Word Scramble

1. feet
6. children

2. mile
7. night

3. white
8. car

4. until
9. side

5. sea
10. walk

212. Find the Words B

```
R L P D T T O G I Z N W
Q Y Z W K F E E T S M O
L M C K A H Q R I I L U
N L H K J L I U J D U A
O M I L E G K T U E A O
P S L O P T H S N R C S
Q X D Y W S E D T O A N
M Z R N V G X C I J R I
A S E R U T R A L A C D
Y I N Y Z W H I T E E F
E N I G H T S E A M B L
Q U N S B A R B D K O E
```

Unit 27 Answer Key

217. Find the Words A

```
P  U  C  B  E  G  A  N
P  V  R  I  V  E  R  I
T  H  C  A  R  R  Y  W
H  E  A  R  G  R  O  W
S  T  A  T  E  E  X  M
U  M  F  O  U  R  W  G
O  N  C  E  T  O  O  K
M  Y  B  O  O  K  G  O
```

218. Write the Words in Sentences

1. carry	6. river or book
2. book	7. grow
3. took	8. state or river
4. hear	9. Once
5. four	10. began

219. Find the Words B

```
F  R  K  P  C  H  I  L  M  D  R  O
R  T  A  F  L  G  R  O  W  Z  I  N
E  O  O  L  O  M  E  O  R  A  T  V
D  O  C  C  E  U  R  O  P  M  Y  X
A  K  R  A  I  S  R  B  O  O  K  G
I  N  P  R  L  C  I  R  N  W  E  H
K  B  E  R  P  G  M  G  C  A  E  E
L  M  E  Y  L  H  A  T  E  O  R  A
D  O  S  G  E  S  S  T  A  T  E  R
R  V  I  E  A  K  A  O  E  D  O  D
E  A  S  A  C  N  T  R  I  V  E  R
N  V  X  G  D  N  Q  G  F  N  B  N
```

220. Choose the Correct Words

1. state	6. river
2. carry	7. grow
3. book	8. took
4. four	9. hear
5. began	10. once

221. Just-for-Fun Missing Letters

1. carry	6. began
2. state	7. once
3. took	8. hear
4. book	9. grow
5. river	10. four

Unit 28 Answer Key

nd the Words A

```
C M S E C O N D F H
R E N O U G H E A T
Z D A P O S T O P C
M I S S P U Q U G F
G O Q Y U S U C E A
B X A A T P A J S Y
J D A P L K R Z F P
N V W I T H O U T O
L A T E D W A T C H
O I D E A F A C E O
```

227. Choose the Correct Words

1. watch	6. enough
2. stop	7. idea
3. second	8. late
4. face	9. miss
5. eat	10. without

225. Write the Words in Sentences

1. eat or watch or stop	5. enough
2. idea or watch	6. stop
3. watch	7. face or watch
4. miss or watch or stop	8. second
	9. late
	10. without

228. Just-for-Fun Anagrams

Students do activity individually.

226. Find the Words B

```
Y Q H W X J H M L R I U
X W A T C H F A M I C
U F I C N K W E O S K O
P G D T S L V E T E S V
O F R E H A A I C C E F
H U A W B O R T I O S L
E Z X C A Y U R E N T N
M I S H E C I T E D O E
O D R L A M O K D L P O
X E E A T J E N O U G H
Q A O G I R N P O M Q B
T F I O V Q V J I C V E
```

Unit 29 Answer Key

231. Find the Words A

```
Q D L Z I Z V Y H J M K
G X B P M A B O V E M M
H I N D I A N F A R Z L
A G L E T U X R L Y E P
M C T H M Y H U N Q O H
P O K P Y H D N N S V A
H U R E A L M O S T C A
R U T H C U T Q V U Y E
M R V B Y X L A C F Q J
S L I E K G R M A R H R
T K G S O M E T I M E S
G I R L M O U N T A I N
```

234. Choose the Correct Words

1. almost	6. above
2. sometimes	7. Indian
3. girl	8. cut
4. far	9. real
5. mountain	10. let

232. Write the Words in Sentences

1. Sometimes	6. mountain
2. let	7. above
3. far	8. almost
4. cut	9. girl
5. Indian	10. real

235. Just-for-Fun Mystery Words

1. sometimes	6. mountain
2. let	7. Indian
3. girl	8. above
4. real	9. almost
5. cut	10. far

233. Find the Words B

```
Z O X F R E Q U O X O A
P R B V F Y L C U T P E
O S E T Z A K P L W I L
Y O C A O L R E I V W O
N M E S L M J I N U G P
B E C D X O A W D T I Q
M T O Y R S Q O I Z R N
M I D I P T T F A H L E
L M O U N T A I N L T S
K E C Z Y B Y L A W R V
N S O G A B O V E R T S
B R U H J W Z R G T Q I
```

Unit 30 Answer Key

Find the Words A

```
B O D Y S O N G H
O M U S I C M E N
A Z Y F O G Y F W
O A H J K K T V W
A C O L O R Y H G
U T W F A M I L Y
M O Y O U N G W Q
T A L K S O O N P
L E A V E L I S T
```

241. Choose the Correct Words

1. body
2. song
3. young
4. talk
5. music
6. soon
7. list
8. family
9. color
10. leave

239. Write the Words in Sentences

1. family or list
2. song
3. color
4. talk or leave
5. body
6. leave
7. young
8. music
9. soon
10. list

242. Just-for-Fun Letter Squares

1. talk
2. song
3. leave
4. music
5. young
6. body
7. soon
8. list
9. family
10. color

240. Find the Words B

```
F G A C O I N R R I N M
C R I D L E A V E M W N
L N S B A I A S R C I O
E H O I R L S O T O A M
X S O N G I F T O L L G
H P N Y U C Z N L O A A
J C H M K E H C B R Y T
A T A B U L I F O H O G
D A W C D S E G D R U O
E L P F A M I L Y T N K
V K O S E R P C Q I G N
C U H T B R E K F E S H
```